Twayne's United States Authors Series

Sylvia E. Bowman, *Editor*

INDIANA UNIVERSITY

Zane Grey

ZANE GREY

By CARLTON JACKSON
Western Kentucky University

 218

Twayne Publishers, Inc. :: New York

MANUFACTURED IN THE UNITED STATES OF AMERICA BY
UNITED PRINTING SERVICES, INC.
NEW HAVEN, CONN.

FOR PAT

Preface

Zane Grey was known primarily as a writer of Romantic novels of the American West. His characters often were stereotyped, and his prose sometimes was forced and stilted. Since he authored eighty-five books, occasional inferior writing could be expected. Thus, any fair assessment of Grey's work must rest upon his total publishing record. His works have sold over forty million copies in twenty different languages. He had so many unpublished book manuscripts (some had appeared in serial form in magazines) at the time of his death in 1939 that his publisher, Harper & Row, decided to publish one a year until the supply was exhausted. The last one, *Boulder Dam*, appeared in 1963.

Grey regarded Romanticism as tantamount to love. The Great West encouraged "love affairs" with Nature, especially the wild beauty of open spaces, and with rugged individualism. Grey wrote about the Westerner in the way that non-Westerners wanted him to. He developed a Western mythology that, along with the frontier theory of Frederick Jackson Turner, helped to turn the West into the most romanticized area of the United States. The West, to Grey, was just as much an idea in the United States as it was a geographical region. Perhaps the West did not offer the charm with which Grey, Owen Wister, and others endowed it, but that was not the most important point. The significant thing was that Americans *thought* the West had all these qualities.

Since it is possible for entire nations, as well as individuals, to have "psychological props," it was what Americans thought of the West that really counted. The German leader, Otto von Bismarck, once said, in effect, "If you think something is true, it is." Thus, images that people have of an area often constitute its reality; and in "image-making" Grey excelled. It would be incorrect to claim that Grey built *only* a Western mythology. His characterizations may have done that, but his descriptions did not. He adopted the novelist's license of creating his own characters and of giving them the traits he wanted them to have. Many of his characters were not true to life; they had super-human qualities that few real people could approach.

Despite this weakness in characterization, Grey's descriptions of the West were accurate; and most of the major events he talked about were historically authentic. Thus Grey chronicled an entire era of American history, and it was this aspect of his work that was most important. In *The U.P. Trail*, for example, he wrote knowingly about the corrupt machinations of the Credit Mobilier; in *The Desert of Wheat* and *The Call of the Canyon*, he described the swiftly changing social scene in America and the shabby treatment given to veterans of World War I. In addressing himself to historical and contemporary problems, Grey was much more, therefore, than a mere "writer of Westerns."

Grey's career led almost automatically to the question: can an author be excellent and popular at the same time? Many people felt that the two qualities were inevitably divorced—that only time could produce popularity for an excellent writer. In respect to Grey, his novels from 1915 through the mid-1920's were on the best-selling lists, with only the Bible and McGuffey's readers outselling him. This fact certainly attests to his popularity. If the mark of excellence depends on time, Grey's books in the 1960's were still selling over a million copies a year. They continued to be models followed by many movie and television shows, and popular abridgements of his works sold rapidly in England and the Commonwealth countries.

Perhaps the continuing fascination of Grey throughout the 1960's was, in part, the lure of escapism—fiction that does not attempt to do anything but entertain. The Grey abridgements omitted many descriptive passages included in the early editions, leaving mostly the action; and this magnified action may have kept Grey popular. The abridgements, partially eliminating historical settings and descriptions, and stressing action, did not represent attempts to edit out inferior parts of his work; they were merely an adjustment to changing reading habits.

It could also have been Grey's treatment of a minority group that partially caused his readership to flourish. In our own era, much stress has been placed on equal and humanitarian treatment of minorities. Grey did this for the American Indian long before the concept became fashionable. Grey cared about the things he described in his pages, and his sincerity came across to the reader, and still does.

The following chapters attempt to explain how and why Grey

became a writer of Western novels and to show the significance of his writing to American literature. No full-scale biography of Grey is attempted; his personal life is discussed only as it relates to his publishing record. The novels have been categorized, and representative novels of each category are discussed in some detail, while others are mentioned only to show thematic development and points of view. An effort has been made to give a critical assessment of Grey's works and to establish a rationale in which his contributions to literature may be evaluated.

I have not included in this study the two novels by Grey that are still unpublished: *The Reef Girl* and *The Young George Washington*. Nor have I dealt with Helen Cody Westmore and Zane Grey, *Last of the Great Scouts*, for Grey wrote only the foreword and the conclusion of this book. Some reports claim that Grey wrote a chapter in a book called *The Woman Accused*. Also, there is talk among Grey fans of a "lost" novel, *Heart of the Desert*. I have made no effort to treat these here.

Many people helped me write this book, and to each I am grateful. Zane Grey's family was most cooperative and hospitable. I wish to thank Mrs. Betty Grosso, Mr. Romer Grey, and Dr. Loren Grey for their kindnesses. Mrs. Eleanora Evans was gracious to me and my work, and I am appreciative.

My friends and colleagues, Professors Mary Clarke of the English Department, and Lowell Harrison of the History Department, at Western Kentucky University, read the manuscript and saved me from numerous pitfalls. I am, of course, responsible for any remaining errors.

The staffs of several libraries went out of their way to facilitate my task. The personnel at the Library of Congress, University of Texas Library, New York Public Library, and Bowling Green, Kentucky, Library were especially helpful and friendly. Mr. Joseph Slade, editor of *The Markham Review*, helped me acquire some important letters. Harper & Row Publishers kindly allowed access to some Grey material. Western Kentucky University History Chairman, J. Crawford Crowe, helped by putting typing facilities at my service. I wish to thank him, as well as my students, Betty Mount and Sharon Buchanan, for their efficiency.

Two men were of great assistance in my study of Grey. Mr. Norris Schneider of Zanesville, Ohio, curator of the Zane Grey Exhibit, put his knowledge of Grey at my disposal, as did the Reverend G. M. Farley of Williamsport, Maryland, editor of *The Zane Grey Collector*. To both men I am grateful. Research grants from Western Kentucky University aided the project. To each member of the Research Committee: thank you.

I must thank Dr. Sylvia E. Bowman, editor of TUSAS, for giving me the opportunity to "live," as it were, for the last several months with such a truly fascinating person as Zane Grey. Finally, I am pleased once again, to express gratitude to my family, Pat, Beverly, Daniel, and Matthew, for their patience and understanding.

CARLTON JACKSON

Western Kentucky University
Bowling Green

Contents

Chronology

1872 Zane Grey, born in Zanesville, Ohio, January 31; parents, Lewis and Josephine Gray.

1888- Dentistry and baseball in Ohio. Offered a baseball scholar-
1892 ship at the University of Pennsylvania.

1896 Was graduated from the University of Pennsylvania.

1896- Dental practice in New York City, 100 West 74th Street.
1903

1902 Met Miss Lina Elise Roth (Dolly), his future wife.

1902 "A Day on the Delaware" in *Recreation*, his first published article,

1903 *Betty Zane*, first published book.

1905 Married Lina Roth.

1907 Went West with C. J. "Buffalo" Jones.

1910 *The Heritage of the Desert*, his first major success in the field of literature.

1912 *Riders of the Purple Sage*.

1907- Traveled extensively through Arizona, New Mexico, Cuba,
1917 and Mexico gathering material for his novels.

1917 *Wildfire*.

1918 Set up a permanent homestead in California.

1918 *The U.P. Trail*.

1919 Crossed Death Valley for the first time.

1919 Wrote his first major fishing book, *Tales of Fishes*.

1921 Returned to home-town of Zanesville, Ohio, as a celebrated author.

1922 *To the Last Man*.

1924 Fishing at Nova Scotia. Bought *Fisherman I*.

1925 *The Vanishing American* published; this book, Grey said, he wanted to be remembered by.

[13]

1926   *Under the Tonto Rim*.

1926- Paid periodic visits to New Zealand and the South Seas.
1929

1930   Twentieth anniversary of Grey's affiliation with Harper's
       Publishing Company. Hailed as the most sought after
       writer in America.

1930   *The Shepherd of Guadaloupe*.

1931   Bought *Fisherman II*.

1937   Suffered stroke while fishing on North Umpqua River,
       Oregon.

1938   Fishing trip to Australia.

1939   *Western Union*. Last of Greys' novels published in his
       lifetime.

1939   Died at his home in Altadena, California, October 23, of
       a heart attack.

Zane Grey

CHAPTER 1

Genesis of a Writer

Spectacular success for Zane Grey was probably the last thing that any citizen of Zanesville, Ohio, in the 1870's and 80's would have predicted. By all accounts Grey was a precocious lad who pulled up neighbors' tulip beds, picked on smaller boys, and dipped girls' pigtails into his inkwell at school. Early in life, he developed into a more avid fisherman than scholar. Grey often remarked that the best place in the world was Dillon's Falls on the Licking River. After Dillon's Falls, Grey was fond of the area under the "Y" bridge in Zanesville, which spans the junction of the Muskingum and Licking Rivers. Fishing to Grey was an obsession; he found peace and comfort in the solitude that the habit gave him. In later life, he held many of the world's fishing records.

I Early Literary Influences

The thrills of fishing produced in Grey an undying love for the out-of-doors. He roamed with gangs of boys to the fishing spots, to the baseball practice fields, and to a special place—a cave where he and his cohorts cooked, ate, told stories, and wrote. To carry on this clandestine life, utensils were obviously necessary. So the "Terror of the Terrace," as Grey was called by neighbors, took pots and pans and other items from the Grey household on Convers Avenue. It was while patronizing the cave that Grey wrote his first story, at the age of fourteen. Understandably enough, it was called "Jim of the Cave," and it was about a group of misunderstood boys who were trying to win the favor of a "light-haired girl."

His first literary effort, however, was doomed. Grey's father, Dr. Lewis Gray, had wondered for some time about the disappearance of his kitchen paraphernalia. When he discovered that his own son had taken the equipment, he burst into the cave, gave Zane a hiding, and burned the manuscript of "Jim of the Cave." After this incident, Zane restricted his writings mostly

to English assignments in school, a chore that he did not relish.
There had been some instances of Grey's writing poetry. When
he was thirteen, he penned this advice to Anna Oldham:

> Friend Anna
> Remember this and bear in mind
> A good beau is hard to find.
> But if you find one gentle and gay
> Hang to his coat tail night and day
> But if your hands should choose to slip
> Catch another and let him rip.
>
> > Yours truly,
> > Pearl Gray.

Later in Grey's life, he dropped his first name "Pearl" (given
to him by his mother, probably in honor of England's Queen
Victoria who was fond of wearing clothes colored pearl gray) because his readers always thought he was a woman, and started
using his middle name "Zane." At the same time, he substituted
an "e" for the "a" in his last name. Grey was named for his great-
grandfather, Ebenezer Zane, whose wife, Elizabeth, was half-
Indian. From this marriage Grey claimed his inheritance of Indian blood. Colonel Zane defended Fort Henry (present-day
Wheeling, West Virginia) during the American Revolution, and
for his services he received several "military warrants," enabling
him to select plots of land for himself. One such tract was Zanesville, an area later incorporated into the State of Ohio. It was in
that city on January 31, 1872, that the Colonel's great-grandson,
Zane Grey, was born. In several books, Grey listed the year of
his birth as 1875, but records indicate that 1872 was the correct
date.

Though Grey's ardor for literary production was cooled by
the cave incident, he began reading a great deal. His favorite
books were Daniel Defoe's *Robinson Crusoe*, James Fenimore
Cooper's *The Last of the Mohicans*, and a book that Grey said he
knew by heart, Charles McKnight's *Our Western Border* published in 1876.[1] Grey was also intrigued by the publishing ideas
of a man from Brooklyn, Erastus Beadle. In 1858, Beadle started
writing short novels about the Revolution and the Mexican War.
These novelettes, costing one dime each, were melodramatic accounts of soldiers at war, which sold quickly to the young generation. The "dime novel" became one of the major literary expressions in the country. As time went on, Beadle contracted several
authors to write stories for him. Two such writers interesting to

Grey were Prentiss Eingrahm and Edward L. Wheeler, who wrote about Indians and border warfare, among other things.

Popular writing of a historical nature was the literature Grey enjoyed most as a boy. This genre was not sufficient to please his teachers, so Grey had only a mediocre record as a student. Later in life, his wife taught him the finer points of English grammar and also an appreciation of authors like Victor Hugo, Edgar Allan Poe, Rudyard Kipling, John Ruskin, Charles Darwin, Alfred Tennyson, and Matthew Arnold. But when Grey was a student at Moore School in Zanesville, sophisticated literature was the last thing on his mind. He dreamed of Dillon's Falls and big fish, homeruns and shut-outs, the freedom of wide open spaces, and "light-haired girls." These diversions helped Grey later, but they drove his mathematics and music teachers to distraction.

Grey's music teacher suddenly stopped the chorus during a session one day and told Grey to be quiet. Grey, who retorted that he had a good singing voice, demanded to know why the teacher had not taught him to use it. The teacher replied that he had attempted to teach Grey how to sing. Responding to this claim, Grey averred that the teacher had certainly given special lessons to some of the girls in the class. Grey climaxed the incident by closing his music book, slamming it against the wall, and swearing that he would never study music again.[2]

Such impertinence in the statement of opinion served Grey well in his future career, but it produced some uncomfortable moments for him as a teen-ager. Perhaps it was audacity of one kind or another that caused Grey's father to treat him sometimes in a punitive fashion. For example, his father, who liked to take afternoon naps, often required Zane to fan his face to keep off the flies. Frequently, Zane fanned until his father was sound asleep, then he put a newspaper over the elder man's face and slipped off. Sometimes this ruse did not work, to Zane's keen disappointment. The father, a great lover of snow, eagerly looked forward to the first blasts of winter. When snow fell, one of Zane's duties was to go out with a bucket and collect the white stuff so his father could eat it. If the snow was not fresh enough, Zane had to make several trips to satisfy his father.

II Dentistry and Baseball

Grey's father was determined that his son become a dentist. Hence, Zane spent much time working on vulcanized teeth—removing plaster of paris from them and polishing them on a lathe. When the family moved to Columbus, Ohio, Zane started an informal dentistry practice at the little town of Frazeysburg. Apparently the work was not completely abhorrent, for Grey recorded in his autobiography, *The Living Past*, "I had all the young girls in the country coming for dental work whether they needed it or not." In due time the Ohio Dental Association became interested in Grey's activities of pulling, filling, and cleaning teeth—especially since Grey was still a minor and was not a graduate of any dental school. A state dental inspector studied Grey's career, chased him out of the business, but predicted a brilliant future for him—in dentistry.

Grey's dental work helped to keep his right arm strong, the same arm that made him a baseball pitcher of professional quality. Zane and his brother, Romer, were always fond of the game; but they did not play in earnest until the family moved to Columbus. In the town of Baltimore, Ohio, which Grey visited on dental business, he pitched a game for the local team whose opponents that day were from Jacktown, Ohio. Baltimore got several runs, and Grey's superb pitching kept the Jacktown team scoreless. Suddenly the umpire, who had been brought to the game by Jacktown, shouted: "Game called! Nine to nothing! Favor Jacktown! Baltimore pitcher uses a crooked ball!" Grey was, of course, delivering his curve ball which he had perfected. The pitcher for Jacktown, however, apparently had never heard of a curve ball, for he went after Grey in a fashion that caused Zane to leave the playing field in haste. After the Jacktown incident, Grey played for the Town Street Club in Columbus and also for the Capitol team. Many of these games formed the basis for Grey's later stories about baseball such as *The Young Pitcher* and *The Red-Headed Outfield*. While Grey was playing for an amateur league, a baseball scout offered him a scholarship at the University of Pennsylvania. This offer posed an important decision for Grey, one that affected his career as a dentist and a writer.

When Grey matriculated at the University of Pennsylvania, he discovered that he would have to pass freshman tests with an average of sixty before he was eligible to play baseball. At this point, Grey undoubtedly regretted the nonchalance with which he had treated his high school subjects, for every test he took was returned with a grade below sixty. So it was a disheartened Grey who walked into Professor Robert Formad's class in histology to take the final examination. He had probably "crammed" for this test since he knew it was his last chance. To Grey's great amazement and pleasure, he scored ninety-nine on the histology test! The professor told him his good grade was in large part, attributable to his drawing ability—an ability that served Grey later as he illustrated some of his books. Grey, in his unpublished autobiography, said of the histology test: "That 99 mark brought my average up beyond passing, and it was responsible for my baseball career, my finding myself in the East, and surely led to my literary career."

As a student at Pennsylvania, Grey was restless. He recorded in his autobiography that he could not concentrate on lectures: "My thoughts wandered afar, if not in green fields and quiet woods, then to dreams of what might come true. In truth, I was a poor student." Grey's prowess on the baseball field rather than his academic record got him through the University of Pennsylvania. A reason, perhaps, why he disliked the academic side of the university was the dental curriculum into which his father forced him. In 1896, Grey was graduated from Pennsylvania, but he expressed doubts that he had truly earned a diploma. Shortly after his college days ended, Grey established a dental practice in New York City.

One may wonder why Grey, the great lover of the out-doors that he was, chose New York as a place to practice his profession. One possible explanation was that he yearned for financial independence, and New York could give it to him quicker than other places. He wanted the leisure to follow his own interests, and money was essential. Dentistry, therefore, must always have been treated by Grey as a "stop-gap" occupation, one that would suffice until he could return to his beloved fishing grounds. He made several important contacts in New York; some made him popular, and others helped launch him on a literary career. For example, he played baseball with an Orange, New Jersey team. His fans attended the games, not just to see him hit home runs, but to get their teeth attended to on the playing field! Also, Grey joined a camp-fire club in New York, an organization devoted to big-game hunting. Through this affiliation, he managed to get his short article "A Day on the Delaware" (1902) printed in *Recreation* magazine. This small success only whetted his appetite for writing, and he became ever more entranced with the possibilities.

Grey's stay in New York from 1896 to 1903 was one of the most significant periods of his life. He could not refrain from comparing the side-walk jungles with the pristine beauty he remembered from his youth. Homesickness tended to magnify the woodlands and streams of Zanesville and Lackawaxen, Pennsylvania, to which most of his family had moved after its sojourn in

Columbus. Throughout, his writings were constant contrasts between the effete East and the manly West. These contrasts were developed in Grey's mind long before he headed for the Western regions.

Quite frequently, Dr. Grey felt the call of open spaces so intensely that he locked up his office and headed for the family home at Lackawaxen; and on such an outing in 1902 Grey met his future wife. He and some friends were canoeing on the Delaware River near Lackawaxen when they saw some girls around a cabin on the bank, and naturally they flirted with the young ladies. One of them was Miss Lina Roth of New York City. Grey called her Dolly. Dolly taught Grey, during the courtship prior to their marriage in 1905, to appreciate the subtle beauty of the English language.

III The Ohio River Trilogy

His friendship with Dolly may have caused Grey to venture into writing his first book in 1902. He had wished long enough, he had studied sufficiently, and he had the moral support of Dolly, so he yielded to his writing instinct. During the day, he labored half-heartedly over teeth; at night, he worked exuberantly on his book. He wrote his first novel "in a dingy flat, on a kitchen table under a flickering light. All of one Winter I labored over it, suffered, and hoped, was lifted up, and again plunged into despair." Under conditions such as these, only his writer's faith and belief in ultimate success sustained him. Grey *had* to write; had he not he would have been miserably unhappy for the rest of his life. Even if that first book had never been published, the writing of it gave him the miserable joy of being a writer, and helped him to escape the drudgery of dentistry.

Grey's "masterpiece" of 1903 was *Betty Zane*, the first book of his Ohio River trilogy. *Betty Zane* was set in the American Revolution, and its ultimate success caused Grey to be compared with James Fenimore Cooper as a recorder of historical events. Grey had heard stories all of his life about how his great-grandfather Ebenezer Zane had defended Fort Henry against Indian attacks. Colonel Zane, a native Virginian, took "tomahawk possession" of the place in 1769 by blazing a few trees with a tomahawk to show ownership. Grey stated in a preface to *Betty Zane* that he had derived his story from an old diary of the Colonel that had been hidden away in a picture frame. The diary was, however, as fictitious as some of the characters in the story. Even if the diary had existed, it is doubtful that it could have been hidden successfully in a picture frame.

Betty Zane, however, was mostly about real places, real events, and real people. Colonel Zane actually existed, as did Betty, Lewis Wetzel, the Girty brothers, and several Wyandotte, Shawnee, and Seneca Indians such as Pipe, Wingenund, and Cornplanter. *Betty Zane* was an example of a good historical novel for the time, place, and the main events were authentic. Grey employed dramatic license on occasion to make his story more realistic than it was. Its total effect made readers aware of their heritage, and showed how one incident of the Revolution helped produce a nationalistic experience.

The story opened with Colonel Zane's return from a hunting trip. At supper that night, Captain Boggs and his daughter Lydia were guests; and Boggs stated his fears of an impending Indian attack. While the two men conversed about this grave subject, Lydia and the Colonel's sister Betty indulged in girlish talk about the arrival in the neighborhood of a young man, a Southerner, named Alfred Clarke. Early in the novel, Grey let the reader know that Betty and Clarke would have a romance, though their initial meetings did not indicate such. Clarke showed sincerity in defending patriot land from the British by leaving a comfortable home in Virginia and coming to the untamed border to fight for the American side. The Colonel gave him an important position in protecting the fort; and, in carrying out his duties, he ran afoul of Betty's desires to wander wherever she wished.

Isaac Zane, the Colonel and Betty's brother, showed up at the fort, having escaped from several years' captivity by the Wyandottes. Through Isaac's contact with various Indians, and through his betrothal to an Indian Princess, Myeerah, he knew that the British were planning a union with the Hurons, Delawares, Shawnees, and other tribes. Despite this news, the Zane household was a scene of festivity in celebration of Isaac's return. Lurking in the background on this and other events at the Zane house was the mysterious figure of Lewis Wetzel, who had been given many names by the Indians. To the Delawares he was "Deathwind"; to the Shawnees, "Longknife"; and to the Hurons, "Destroyer." Wetzel was a professional Indian hunter. His family had been slaughtered in an Indian raid, and he had vowed undying vengeance. When he stalked an Indian, the legend was that a low moaning wind swept through the forest just before he struck. Lewis loved Betty, but he knew that his "occupation" forever prevented him from winning her hand.

The joy of the Zanes over Isaac's return was short-lived, for he was again taken by the Indians. Confronting his fiancée, Myeerah, Isaac begged her to return to Fort Henry with him. She refused; so "White Eagle," as Isaac was called, decided to abandon immediate escape attempts and gather information of possible use to the citizens of Fort Henry. Grey used Isaac's captivity to discuss the American Indian, his thesis being that the Indians were not barbarians until the white man made them so. He wrote of the several betrayals of Indians by white men that had turned the native American into a hostile force. Grey employed this theme in dozens of his later novels. Grey may have portrayed Wetzel as the personification of glory, but Grey's sympathy was with the Indians.

Isaac escaped again, only to lose himself hopelessly in the forest. He was finally found by Cornplanter, the Seneca Chief, at whose camp plans were made to torture and kill Isaac. It was here that Isaac first met the notorious white renegade, Simon Girty. The traitor took a perverse pleasure in telling Isaac that nothing could save him, and he embellished his opinion by relating the awful end that had come recently to Colonel William Crawford and his soldiers at the hands of the Indians. At the crucial moment, however, Myeerah appeared with a group of Indians and saved Isaac. Then Isaac, in gratitude, offered to return to the Indian camp as Myeerah's husband. But the maiden, who wanted only to please her lover, traveled to Fort Henry with Isaac, where the two were married.

At the fort, celebrations were again in order. But there was still an overhanging dread in the reports of an impending attack. The novel reached its climax when a concerted British-Indian onslaught was launched against Fort Henry. During the fight, the defenders of the fort ran out of gunpowder. Betty Zane ran from the fort to Colonel Zane's cabin to get a supply of the precious material, which she carried in an apron slung over her shoulder. Both to and from the cabin, Betty ran through a hail of bullets and arrows; and her heroic dash—historically accurate—saved the fort.

After the fort was saved, Alfred and Betty were married, a fictitious event which occurred only in the novel. Peace with the Indians resulted largely from the union between Isaac and Myeerah. Colonel Zane, who got a land patent from the government for his services, became an important landowner. Only the Indian, as Grey noted, was neglected in the post-revolutionary progress: "The Indian is almost forgotten; he is in the shadow;

his songs are sung; no more will he sing to his dusky bride; his deeds are done; no more will he boast of his all-conquering arm or of his speed like the Northwind; no more will his heart bound at the whistle of the stag, for he sleeps in the shade of the oaks, under the moss and the ferns."

Betty Zane was a product of family stories and a sense of history. The novel laid the groundwork for two more books by Grey about Ohio River country—indeed, that one novel inspired another seemed to become a Grey trademark, for many of his Western novels, the ones for which he is best remembered, were written in sequels. However, Grey learned after he had completed *Betty Zane* the difference between writing a book and getting it published. He wearily carried his manuscript from one publisher to another, only to be turned down. Finally—and this was where Grey's dental practice paid off—he borrowed money from a patient[3] and had the novel published at his own expense. The title page read: "Betty Zane by P. Zane Grey. Cover design, letters and illustrations by the author."

Although *Betty Zane* was not an immediate financial success, its publication led Grey to a number of decisions; and, the first was to abandon dentistry. The second was to return to Zanesville to receive the acclaim of his friends and neighbors. On this visit in April, 1904, he announced that henceforth his life was to be devoted "exclusively to literature," and he promised two more books about Wetzel. The third thing that *Betty Zane* did to Grey was to lead him to the altar. In November, 1905, he and Dolly were married in New York; and they established residence on the banks of the Delaware River in Lackawaxen, Pennsylvania. There, Dolly continued to teach Zane the uses of verbs and nouns; there he also toiled day and night over two more books and several short pieces. That he was making little money on *Betty Zane* did not bother him. He was now an author; and, though he had to borrow money to buy groceries, he had faith that all would be well.

Because of *Betty Zane*, Grey came into contact with Daniel Murphy, agent for the United Literary Press, and with many others. The association between Grey and Murphy was a long and fruitful one. Murphy liked Grey from the first: "You are so complex, so multi-sided, so sensitive that I never attempt to judge you by my simple standards."[4]

Betty Zane also caused dozens of citizens to write to Grey or his publishers. R. B. Brown of the *Zanesville Courier* told the Francis Press: " . . . I confess to great astonishment at the distinct literary ability he has displayed."[5] Mrs. Fannie Burns wrote to Grey's father extolling *Betty Zane*. A glimpse into Grey's relationship with her was seen as she signed herself as Grey's "former teacher and present friend."[6] Inevitably, Grey received letters disputing the geographical facts of *Betty Zane*. Grey was informed that one does not go "down" the river from Fort Henry to Fort Pitt; one goes "Up!"[7] Regardless of whether the letters about *Betty Zane* were friendly or not, Grey gloried in all the interest he had caused by his literary creation.

In 1906, A. L. Burt accepted *Spirit of the Border*, the second novel of the Ohio River trilogy, which continued the story of Lewis Wetzel who now had a partner, Jonathan Zane, brother of Betty and Ebenezer. He also had two more names given him by the Indians: *Le vent de la Mort* and *Atelang*. Wetzel and Jonathan conducted their relentless war against the Indians, but Ebenezer had compassion for the Redman: "Seldom had the rights of the Redman been thought of. The settler pushed onward, plodding, as it were, behind his plow with a rifle. He regarded the Indian as little better than a beast; he was easier to kill than to tame. How little the settler knew the proud independence, the wisdom, the stainless chastity of honor, which belonged to many Indian Chiefs!"

The center of action in the novel was a Moravian mission called the Village of Peace. In their efforts to convert the Indians, the ministers antagonized the chief villain of the story, Jim Girty, brother of Simon. Wetzel urged the head missionary, Mr. Wells, to abandon the mission; if he did not, he would risk jeopardizing the lives of all the people in it. Wells was grateful for Wetzel's help; but, since he still regarded him only as an "Indian-killer," he would not move. At this point, Wetzel gave an explanation of practical Christianity: "No, I ain't a Christian, an' I am a killer of Injuns . . . I don't know nothin' much 'cept the woods an' fields, an' if there's a God fer me He's out thar under the trees an' grass . . . I advised you to go back to Fort Henry, because if you don't go now the chances are against your ever goin'. Christianity or no Christianity, such men as you hev no bisness in these woods." Many times in his future novels, Grey expounded and enlarged on this pragmatic view of Christianity.

Wells, anxious to stay at the mission, entreated Captain David Williamson to protect him. Williamson argued that the Indians and missionaries wanted to sacrifice themselves, so he would not offer any help. Besides, of Williamson's men, only eighteen said they would fight for the Christian Indians. There occurred then a most fearful massacre of the Village of Peace, conducted by Jim Girty and his Indian allies. They set upon the Christian Indians as they were praying and singing hymns in the chapel. This historically accurate event accounted for the death of sixty-two Indian adults and thirty-four Indian children. Only two boys escaped the cruel blow.[8]

The climax of the story came when Wetzel confronted the evil Girty at Beautiful Spring, nailed him to a tree with his knife, and left Girty in agony to spill out his life's blood. As soon as Wetzel's deed was done, he turned around and saw his old enemy Wingenund in the shadows. Wingenund had been converted to Christianity, and his daughter had married a white man. Wetzel finally gave in to the urgings of his white companions, and spared Wingenund. Thus, the story ended. Some critics objected to the excessive violence of *The Spirit of the Border*. Grey, however, would not apologize for the book's brutality; for brutality was the mark of the border.[9]

The final book of the trilogy was *The Last Trail*. In it, the Indian problem had been solved; and white rustlers, led by Bing Leggitt and Simon Girty, caused most of the trouble. Wetzel's and Jonathan Zane's last mission was to clear out the horse thieves before the border could be truly civilized. There were scattered reminiscences in *The Last Trail* of the events in the first two books: Betty Zane's dash for the gunpowder was now legendary, and Captain Williamson's failure to protect the Christian Indians was related at one hearth after another; indeed, it was said that Williamson and his men carried out the massacre themselves! This account was the true one.

Grey used more description in this book than in its two predecessors. He described the inner conflict that comes to a borderman when he falls in love. Jonathan met Helen Sheppard, and loving her seemed unavoidable: "He realized that men had always turned, at some time in their lives, to women even as the cypress leans toward the sun. The weakening of the sterner stuff in him; this softening of his heart, and especially the inquiettude, lack of joy and harmony in his old pursuit of the forest trails bewildered him, and troubled him some. Thousands of times his borderman's trail had been crossed, yet never to his sorrow until now when it had been crossed by a woman." It was, of course, most convenient for Jonathan to start thinking of love and marriage as his work in clearing up the border slowed to a stop. The story ended with the destruction of the horse thieves and with all of the principal characters getting married except

Wetzel, for whom marriage would have been completely out of harmony with his nature. Thus, the Western Virginia border had gone through all of its stages—wilderness, Indians, white rustlers, civilization—and all of its characters had passed into history. Grey could now turn his attention elsewhere.

Grey's reliance on James Fenimore Cooper was evident in the Ohio River trilogy, for he believed, like Cooper, that the truths of history could be taught in a work of fiction as well as in a history book. Likely, too, was the influence of Grey's favorite book as a youth, *Our Western Border*. The trilogy was a test of Grey's fortitude. He fought odds in writing it that would have been considered insurmountable by many other writers. He was so confident of his future as a writer when the reading public became familiar with his work that he paid the publishing expenses himself for his first novel and practically gave away the next two.

By 1905 Grey had drawn up a list of "rules for my literary work." He filled a diary with procedures to read ("study the felicity of words"), to observe ("in everything there is always something undiscovered. Find it."), to think ("train the mind to think earnestly."), and to describe ("the object of description is not so much to tell the truth as to give an impression of truth.")[10] He constantly studied the technical aspects of writing, depending primarily in this respect upon the works of Clayton Hamilton and J. H. Gardiner. Grey had the desire to write and, he believed, the ability. All he needed was the opportunity.

The opportunity came one day in 1907 when Grey made the acquaintance of a man some of his friends had mentioned to him. That man was Charles Jesse "Buffalo" Jones, a well-known Westerner, who was in New York to show films of the wild life in Yellowstone Park. Grey suggested that he go with Jones to Arizona on a hunting trip and write about the experiences. Before giving his consent, Jones needed evidence that Grey could write, so Grey gave Jones a copy of *Betty Zane*. As soon as Jones completed reading the book, he cordially invited Grey to accompany him to the West. This invitation opened a new world for Zane Grey.

CHAPTER 2

The Desert Novels

Grey was thrilled at the chance to explore the West with "Buffalo" Jones. He had some misgivings, however, because he did not want to leave Dolly alone. She, believing this was Grey's great opportunity to secure firsthand knowledge of the West that would make his writings accepted by the reading public, insisted that he go.

I The Last of the Plainsmen

The book that Grey wrote about his adventures with Jones was *The Last of the Plainsmen* in 1908. A foundation work, it inspired many of Grey's later settings and events in his western novels. Jones, an intriguing character, who was originally from Illinois, had hunted and killed buffalo for years before concluding that the great bison herds were becoming extinct. Jones laid down his rifle and spent the rest of his life trying to preserve the buffalo. One great hope in his life was to cross-breed the buffalo with black Galloway cattle. The partial success of this experiment was the famous "cattalo,"[1] said to be stronger and tastier than either a buffalo or a steer. Jones, adopting literally the biblical injunction that man have dominion over all the beasts of the earth, had a way with wild animals. He showed his belief in this role by capturing single-handed some Yellowstone Park bears, by stringing them up by their feet on a tree branch, and by spanking them with a pole until they were subordinate to his wishes.[2] People in the East scoffed at reports of such exploits, so Grey proposed to take photographs and write descriptions of Jones's deeds.

The trip with Jones introduced Grey to many of the major landmarks in the West, particularly in Arizona. Mormons guided Grey, Jones, and several other men as they crossed the Painted Desert, traversed the Big and Little Colorado Rivers, went up Buckskin Mountain, fought wildcats, and got caught in sand-

storms and floods. Grey did not long remain a novice in this wild
setting; for when a Mormon gave him a too-spirited horse, Grey
stuck him out, and won the unqualified approval of his associates.
Grey shot a cougar while on a hunt; he had either to shoot the
animal or be injured or possibly killed by it. Becoming an expert horseman and marksman in a short time, he participated
in a chase for wild horses, and marveled at the dexterity of Jones,
sixty-three years old, in trying to capture them.

Grey was enthralled by the Painted Desert. It was not like
his previous mental images of it: "Imagination had pictured the
desert for me as a vast, sandy plain, flat and monotonous. Reality showed me desolate mountains gleaming bare in the sun,
long lines of red bluffs, white sand dunes, and hills of blue clay,
areas of level ground—in all, a many-hued, boundless world in
itself, wonderful and beautiful, fading all around into the purple
haze of deceiving distance" (18). A desert sunrise led him to
ecstasy: "A stream of opal flowed out of the sun, to touch each
peak, mesa, dome, parapet, temple and tower, cliff and cleft
into the new-born life of another day" (245). When the day was
done, "night intervened, and a moving, changing, silent chaos
pulsated under the bright stars. How infinite all this is! How
impossible to understand! I exclaimed" (251).

The magical qualities of the desert and its sunrises and sunsets
fascinated Grey throughout his life. His preoccupation with such
scenes was reflected in his novels; characterization was always
subordinate to setting. Man could never enchant him as the
Grand Canyon could: "man was nothing, so let him be humble.
This cataclysm of the earth, this playground of a river was not
inscrutable; it was only inevitable—as inevitable as nature herself. Millions of years in the bygone ages it had lain serene under
a live moon; it would bask silent under a rayless sun, in the onward edge of time.—It spoke simply, though its words were
grand: 'My spirit is the Spirit of Time, of Eternity, of God. Man
is little, vain, vaunting. Listen. Tomorrow he shall be gone' " (252).

After his travels with Jones, Grey returned to Lackawaxen to
spend several months writing *The Last of the Plainsmen*. It had
some good touches in it, as when Grey described one of Jones's
earlier adventures into the Arctic regions where he tried to capture musk-ox. Much of the book, however, was written in a remi-
niscent, "camp-fire" style, one not likely to attract a wide audience. Besides, at the time Grey tried to publish the book, President
Theodore Roosevelt was on a highly publicized trip to the West.
Naturally, more people were interested in Roosevelt in 1907 and

1908 than in some obscure dentist who was trying to write novels about the American West.

The lack of sales possibilities did not restrain Grey's enthusiasm in writing *The Last of the Plainsmen*. Shortly after he had finished the book, Jones appeared, and together they went to Harper's where Jones had a friend, Mr. Ripley Hitchcock. Grey, assured through this contact that his book would receive careful consideration, was heartened by the prospect of an acceptance. Several days later Grey was invited back to Harpers, where Hitchcock said of *The Last of the Plainsmen*: "I don't see anything in this to convince me you can write either narrative or fiction."[3]

Grey was, of course, plunged into despair over Hitchcock's decision. But from this chastening came a miraculous transformation in Grey as he recorded in an essay, "My Own Life," printed in a 1928 book by Harper's, *Zane Grey: The Man and his Work*: "Suddenly, something marvelous happened to me, in my mind, to my eyesight, to my breast. That moment should logically have been the end of my literary aspirations! From every point of view I seemed lost. But someone inside me cried out: 'He does not know! *They* are all wrong!'" Years later, when Grey was a famous author, this experience must have come back to him incessantly as he suddenly rescued one dejected character after another in his novels and lifted him to the heights. At least for Grey, he knew that such individual catharsis was possible—that victory could be gained from adversity. His critics disbelieved such a thing, saying it was unrealistic; but such victory fascinated nonetheless over forty million people.

As usual, Grey found greatest comfort in Dolly: "Let no man ever doubt the faith and spirit and love of a woman!"[4] She encouraged him to submit *The Last of the Plainsmen* to other publishers. While the manuscript made its rounds, Grey worked busily on another novel about the great American desert. Ultimately, *The Last of the Plainsmen* was accepted by the Outing Publishing Company in New York. A highlight in Grey's career occurred when Jones attended an autograph dinner party and happily signed the book as "the last of the plainsmen." Grey described the event to his friend and agent, Daniel Murphy: "He [Jones] was simply great that night, and the crowd went wild. When my book was delivered each table got up with a roar . . . . Jones . . . talked about the book, and [said] it was the most thrilling and beautiful story ever written about a sporting event. When my turn came the roar that greeted me stunned me. I got up somehow, with nausea, chromatic aberration, diffuse sweating,

prolapsis [*sic*] of the intestines, paralysis of the centers of equilibrium, and what might be called balmastatic globulation of the
oracular function."5

Grey reported later that something of Jones always appeared
in the great fictional characters that Grey created.6 Jones held
a commanding position in Grey's later novel, *The Raiders of
Spanish Peaks*, for example, and in several articles and stories
for boys. *Roping Lions in the Grand Canyon* was essentially a
revised shorter version of *The Last of the Plainsmen*, and *The
Young Forester* and *The Young Lion Hunter* were variants of the
same basic work. Grey's descriptions of his Western tour with
Jones pulsated from the vast panorama of the book to the vivid
closeups of the articles and stories, but what was often described
hurriedly in the book was carefully scrutinized in the short articles and stories. "Lassoing Lions in the Siwash," in *Everybody's
Magazine* of June, 1908, was the first of several articles extracted
from *The Last of the Plainsmen*. As late as 1922, in *Tales of
Lonely Trails*, Grey was still explaining "Buffalo" Jones to the
world.

Despite the tremendous value of "Buffalo" Jones to Grey's
development as a writer of Western novels, it was another man—
Jim Emett—who most influenced Grey. Jim Emett, born in a
covered wagon crossing the plains, spent his entire life on the
desert; five nights out of every seven, Emett slept out doors.
Emett was in trouble in Flagstaff, Arizona when Grey first met
him in 1907; one Saunders had accused him of cattle rustling, and
there was also bad blood between Emett and a man named Dimmick. When Emett and Dimmick ultimately pulled guns on each
other, Grey—either bravely or naïvely—stepped in between
them and stopped the fight. The incident furnished Grey with
much material for his stories.7

Emett, over six-feet tall, had ponderous shoulders, a great
"shaggy" head, and a white beard; and he "gave the impression
of tremendous virility and dignity." He had a strange gift of revelation: " . . . [H]e divined what the desert would come to mean
to me. He . . . [saw] all it was to bring to me."8 Emett, a Mormon, loved and cared for all creatures, including children—of
whom he was the father of eighteen by two different wives.
"Rustlers and horsethieves, outlaws from the notorious Hole in
the Wall—All were welcomed by Jim Emett. He had no fear of
any man. He feared only his God."9 The greatest gift from Emett
to Grey was the habit of silent watching: "Surely, of all the gifts
that have come to me from contact with the West, this one of

sheer love of wilderness beauty, color, grandeur, has been the greatest, the most significant for my work."[10]

II The First Major Success

It was predictable, in view of his Western tour with Jones, that Grey's first major success was a novel about the desert. *The Heritage of the Desert* set the theme of the Romantic novels for which Grey became famous: that of having the West ultimately transform weaklings into strong men, and of building individual character. When he completed the book in 1910, he returned to Harper's, and presented his manuscript to Hitchcock. Days later he was called back to the publishing house, where a smiling Hitchcock pushed one of Harper's famous blue contracts at him— a contract that immediately became a treasured heirloom.

The main character of *The Heritage of the Desert* was twenty-four-year-old John Hare, an Easterner who had come to the West in the 1870's to regain his health and to restore some meaning to his life. In Salt Lake City he was mistaken for a cattleman's spy by outlaws, and thus became a hunted man. Before the chief outlaw, a former Kentuckian named Dene, could find him, Hare was rescued by some Mormons headed by August Naab. One Mormon, Martin Cole, had doubts about playing the Good Samaritan to Hare because Cole did not want to antagonize Dene. When Naab prevailed, Hare stayed with the group. Naab's blessing supper one night caused Hare's early religious thoughts to return. In Connecticut, he had been flippant about religion; but Naab's piety was touching. The incident launched the novel's leading theme: the gentle callings of religion could not destroy evil by a continual policy of appeasement toward bad men. This hard lesson August Naab ultimately came to accept.

In the group of Mormons was Mescal, the young daughter of a Navajo Indian mother and a Spanish father. She had been reared and educated by the Mormons, and was regarded by them as a future wife for Naab's son, Snap.[11] The son, however, was a surly, hard-drinking troublemaker, who proved that good people can sire rotten children. Snap's first wife hated Mescal because of the anticipated marriage, and Snap hated Hare because of the infatuation between the latter and Mescal which grew with each page of the novel.

The antagonisms were brought together in the little settlement of White Sage, which Naab and Hare visited one day for supplies. While the two men were in town, these things happened: Morman Bishop Caldwell "laid hands" on Hare, indicating a proselyting effort; Martin Cole pronounced a malediction on a rancher named Holderness (who wanted to marry Mescal) for cutting off the water supply to desert farmers; Snap won a shoot-out with Jeff Larson over a horse-trading deal; and Naab disarmed Dene for terrorizing Hare, but refused additional violence because of his religion. All of this fast-paced action occurred within the short space of one afternoon. The remainder of the novel was spent, for the most part, in settling all the personal conflicts inspired by that trip to town.

At Naab's ranch, the Blue-Star, from which the roar of the mighty Colorado was heard, the relationship between Naab and Hare drew close. The relationship was, in one instance, man to man because Naab gave Hare important responsibilities to show that he had faith in Hare's masculinity. It was also father to son, as Naab saw Snap slowly reject the old traditions and become a gunman. Naab began to transfer to Hare the affection for his oldest son. Hare's ingratiation of himself to Naab and Mescal produced for him a mortal enemy in Snap Naab. Because of this enmity, Naab assigned Hare to work in the sheep camp, high in the mountains. The strange thing about this assignment was that Mescal accompanied him, and Naab apparently saw no threat as a result to the planned marriage of Snap and Mescal.

In the high areas, many adventures befell Hare. He slowly learned to breathe comfortably in the juniper and black-sage infested grounds, he became expert at driving sheep, he foraged a friendship with the two Indian workers at the camp, he spotted a wild horse—Silvermane—and helped to capture and break it[12] and he killed a bear just a step short of Mescal who was transfixed in horror. He regained his health. He fell in love with Mescal.

Mescal returned Hare's love, but she avoided him because of her Mormon upbringing and her obligation to marry Snap. Hare, infuriated, swore that the marriage would never take place; and he vented his anger by slipping away one day to White Sage where he shot two outlaws, slapped Holderness, and ran down Dene on Silvermane. Despite Hare's escapades, the marriage plans continued. At Christmas time, the sheep camp was abandoned and the crew returned to Blue-Star. On the wedding eve, Mescal slipped away with her horse, Black Bolly; her dog, Wolf; and her faithful Indian servant. She had gone to a place where she did not expect to be found: the Painted Desert!

Searching for Mescal, Naab and Hare employed the services

of Eschtah, the "wise old chief of all the desert Indians," who was Mescal's grandfather. The Indian ordered some braves to look for Mescal, the "desert flower", but he admitted the hopelessness of the situation. Mescal had been called back to the desert by the primitive instincts of her forefathers. As Hare gazed over the desert, seeing in it a deep and majestic nature, eternal and unchangeable, ". . . it was only through Eschtah's eyes that he saw its parched slopes, its terrifying desolateness, its sleeping death." Thus did Hare lament the loss of his beloved Mescal.

In the period following Mescal's flight and after Snap had become foreman at the Holderness Ranch, he slipped up on Hare one day and shot him, though Hare was unarmed. Snap thought he had killed Hare, but Naab nursed the young Easterner back to health. Snap's dastardly deed led Naab to disown him, for Naab was now beginning to realize that, Christian though he was, it would take more than prayers and supplications to stop the domineering tactics of Dene, Holderness, and Snap. Also, Naab absolved Mescal, if she could ever be found, of any duties, matrimonial or otherwise, to Snap.

On the first anniversary of Mescal's departure, Hare was awakened by imagined voices. Arising, he told Naab he was going into the desert. He mounted Silvermane, and found Wolf— Mescal's dog—waiting for him on the bank of the river. When he went into the desert, beset by sandstorms and lack of water, Hare could only put himself at the mercy of his horse and Mescal's dog. At the crucial moment—just when Hare was about to succumb to the elements—he found Mescal! The maiden had lived comfortably until her Indian servant died, and food supplies were exhausted. Together, the lovers headed back to "Blue-Star."

A few days after Mescal's and Hare's return, outlaws appeared under the leadership of Holderness who was now a "sheriff." In the shoot-out that followed, one of Naab's younger sons, Dave, was killed. Three outlaws, including Dene, were slain. Mescal escaped on Silvermane, with Holderness in pursuit. Thus, a showdown of all the contradicting forces was rapidly approaching. That the showdown was certain was indicated by Naab's conversion from an appeaser of outlaws to their sworn foe. He summoned Eschtah and his braves, intending to go after the outlaws on the morrow. During the night, however, Hare slipped away on Black Bolly, Mescal's horse, to do Naab's job for him.

When Hare arrived in the Silver Cup camp, he, to his consternation, found Silvermane tethered outside a cabin. Mescal was inside, a prisoner of Holderness and Snap. The two outlaws quarreled, and Holderness shot Snap through the heart. Plainly, Holderness intended to have Mescal and use her for his own evil purposes. In his secret hiding place, Hare pondered what to do to save Mescal. On into the night he maintained his vigil. Then, an outlaw, "Nebraska," and a masked man, untied Mescal and set her free. Mescal rode swiftly to White Sage where she was placed in the protective custody of Bishop Caldwell. Hare got there just a few minutes ahead of Holderness; the two men drew; Holderness lost.

By this time, a group of irate citizens had gathered, determined to hang every man in the outlaw group. Hare saved "Nebraska" from this fate by telling of the latter's part in helping Mescal escape. Hare also saved the masked rider but not before someone had pulled off his mask. He was none other than Paul Caldwell, the eldest son of the Mormon Bishop! At this point, Naab, the "Old Lion," roared into White Sage, infuriated that Hare had robbed him of his vengeance against Holderness and the outlaws. It took great force to keep Naab from hanging the Bishop's son despite the mitigating circumstances. When Naab had calmed, he gave his blessings to the planned marriage of Hare and Mescal.

The book ended with a grand wedding. Mescal and Hare were married by Naab at Blue-Star under the shade of a cottonwood grove. Eschtah and his Indians, resplendent in their robes were present. Hare and Mescal returned to the old sheep camp high in the mountains where they had discovered their love for each other. This happy ending was the first of almost a hundred that Grey fashioned in his career as a writer of Romantic novels of the American West.

To be sure, *The Heritage of the Desert* was melodramatic in its execution. There were too many coincidences in it, as when Hare heard the call of the desert on the exact anniversary of Mescal's flight from unhappiness, and when Hare conveniently found Mescal being held captive by Holderness and Snap. The novel's themes, however, were universal in their application. There was, for example, the "Good Samaritan" theme, for only love for mankind caused Naab to rescue Hare on the White Sage Trail and keep him from the clutches of Dene. Naab did not know what manner of man Hare was; for all he knew, Hare might have deserved ill treatment from Dene. But Hare was a human being, and "suffering was suffering," no matter the cause, no matter the victim.

Included in the religious aspects of the novel was the almost imperceptible change affecting Mormonism in the 1870's along the Utah-Arizona border. At first, Naab wanted to convert Hare to the Mormon faith; it was his duty, as he saw it, to do so for his Church. Naab also believed that passive goodwill ultimately reigned supreme over evil forces, but the desert taught survival of the fittest for all the creatures who lived on it—and man was not exempt from this requirement, and would have to adjust to conditions. Naab also personified Mormonism in its altering forms in other respects: he relinquished his efforts to convert Hare, but kept him as a son; he came to believe in doctoring bodily injuries; and he became convinced that prayers must sometimes be supplemented by hot lead if law and order were to prevail in the Western regions. This was not the only novel in which Grey wrote about the personal and institutional changes wrought by lawless days in the West. The theme recurred especially in two of his mountain novels, *The Riders of the Purple Sage* and *The Rainbow Trail*. In his treatment of changing Mormonism, Grey put the stamp of historical research on his novels; and he contributed to an understanding of that period in American history.

On the desert, the animal was superior to the human. In his search for Mescal, Hare would not have survived except for the enduring qualities and homing instincts of his horse and Mescal's dog. He put himself at their mercy, and they brought him through. Very little could have been accomplished in the West without burros, dogs, and good horseflesh. Grey came to love the four-footed beasts, even the wild ones, and he imparted this affection to his readers.

The novel also depicted the healing and the edenic qualities of the West. While Hare was in the East, he was sickly with a bad lung. The rarefied atmosphere of the West soon corrected the problem. Also, out West, Hare was expected to be a man, to forget the "soft" life he had led in the East. More important, when the West offered the opportunity to be a man, Hare rose to the challenge, met it in a splendid manner, and received manifold rewards for his efforts. He was just one Grey character out of hundreds who experienced this kind of rejuvenation. This theme, perhaps more than any other, caused Grey to become known in some circles as a Western image builder. If there was a Garden of Eden in this country, Grey let his readers know that it was West of the Mississippi River.

The Heritage of the Desert put Grey on a fairly solid literary

footing. He was quite active immediately after the book's publication—so much so that in June, 1910, he declined an invitation from Boy Scout Director Daniel Beard to visit Forest Lake
near Redding, Connecticut. He said he was working on a juvenile
book (probably *The Young Forester*) that had to be completed
by the end of summer. His improved financial condition was apparent when he wrote," . . . I am interested in places where I
might buy property and locate permanently."[13] Grey, however,
was not yet firmly fixed as an author, despite these positive signs.
His best known book, *Riders of the Purple Sage* (1912) was at
first rejected by Harper's, though *The Heritage of the Desert*
earned a comfortable income. Grey said in 1928, at the height of
his career, that his publication troubles had never ended.[14]

III Wanderer of the Wasteland

By 1910 Grey was earning enough money with his writings to
travel whenever he wished. Thus, he spent about half his time
in Arizona, California, and New Mexico. He took extensive notes
on these trips: and he used them for articles, short stories, and
novels. The desert continued to fascinate him. He crossed the
Painted Desert again, as he had done with "Buffalo" Jones in
1907; he became familiar with the Sonora Desert along the Mexico-Arizona border; and in 1919, with a Norwegian, Sievert
Nielson, he crossed Death Valley in the Mojave Desert. He ob-
served that the desert brought out the primitive instincts of man
which could be used for purposes either good or evil.[15] The desert grasped a peculiar trait a man might have and magnified it a
dozen-fold. To tell the effect of the desert on man was Grey's
objective in a 1923 novel, *Wanderer of the Wasteland*. He was
from January to May, 1919, writing this novel. In manuscript,
it was 170,000 words and 838 pages long. "I do not know what
it is that I have written. But I have never worked so hard on any
book, never suffered so much or so long . . . . The only agony I
feel now is the agony of dread. Have I written what I yearned to
write?"[16]

Wanderer of the Wasteland employed a Cain-Abel conflict as
its major dramatic problem: Adam Larey and his older brother
Guerd quarreled over a woman. In the fight that ensued, Adam
shot Guerd. Thinking he had slain his brother, Adam fled into
the desert to spend many years purging his soul of the guilt that
was in it.

On the desert, Adam lost eighty pounds in one day. He was
near death when a prospector, Dismukes, found him. Later,

however, when Adam was again on his own, his burro stole away with all his food. Thus, survival, the most primitive of man's instincts, became uppermost in his mind. While he endured this trial, Adam learned many secrets of Nature; and one was that all animals lived upon one another. Adam knew that he, like all other creatures, would have to kill to survive; and he ruthlessly stalked partridges, rats, and snakes for something to eat. When Adam did eat, he found that his small amount of food stimulated sharp hunger pangs which themselves were almost fatal, whereas without food at all, there was no pain. He concluded that starving to death was an easy and painless way to die. Just before this happened to Adam, however, he was rescued again, this time by a band of Indians.

In time Adam came to be called "Wansfell the Wanderer." In this role he was a Knight of Shining Armor who rescued fair damsels from the clutches of evil villains. He killed a man named Baldy McKue who abducted and despoiled another man's wife, and he tried, vainly, to save the life of Magdalena Virey. Magdalena and her husband Elliott lived in Death Valley in the path of an avalanche. Magdalena had wronged Elliott in the past, so her travail in Death Valley was one of purgation. She, like Adam Larey, came to the desert to atone for her manifold sins. She was resigned to her fate, for she did nothing as Elliott while trying to activate the avalanche rolled rocks toward their cabin each night. Wansfell begged Magdalena to leave, but she refused; it was as though she welcomed the death that was sure to come. One night Elliott was able to start the avalanche, and before the terrible ordeal ended, both he and his wife were dead. Adam left the scene, taking along a small picture of Magdalena's daughter, Ruth.

On the trail again, Adam thought about God. Dismukes, the prospector, had once told Adam that he would find God on the desert, but Adam doubted the prediction: "You're wrong . . . . I have no religion, no belief. I can't find any hope out there in the desert. Nature is pitiless, indifferent. The desert is but one of her playgrounds. Man has no right there" (143). But Adam's role as benefactor to helpless people caused him ultimately to view things differently. For example, he rescued Genie Linwood from kidnapers, and took her home to a mother dying of consumption. Just before her death, Mrs. Linwood told Adam that he was the answer to her prayers: "What do you call this strength of yours that fulfilled my faith . . . that gave me to God utterly . . . that enables me to die happy . . . that will be the salvation of my child?" (314). Adam's conclusion was pantheistic: "Could God be

Nature—that thing, that terrible force, light, fire, water, pulse—
that quickening of plant, flesh, stone, that dying of all only to re-
new . . . ?" (335). This reconciliation of God and Nature, which
up to Mrs. Linwood's death Adam had denied, showed that
Adam's spiritual powers had kept pace with the physical; he had
not reverted (as most men on the desert do) "to mere unthinking
instinct." His positive qualities came from God, their magnifi-
cation, from the desert. Thus God and Nature came to be one in
Adam Larey's thinking.

Adam and Genie Linwood lived and wandered together for
years, and he had to fight hard to keep from falling in love with
her. To love a woman was out of the question for Adam Larey,
"Wansfell the Wanderer," because he was his brother's slayer,
and had, therefore, to spend his life in contrition. Finally, when
the two went to the little settlement San Ysabel, Genie met a
young man, Gene Blair; and it was clear from the beginning that
they were meant for each other. When Adam met Ruth Virey,
daughter of Magdalena, he did not permit himself to love her;
he left San Ysabel in terrible personal conflict over whether to
return to the desert or go back to Picacho (the scene of strife with
his brother) and take his legal punishment ". . . [T]he I of Adam's
soul was arraigned in pitiless strife with the Me of his body. Like
a wild and hunted creature he roamed the mountain top . . .
there to sit like a stone, to lie on his face, to writhe and fight and
cry in his torment" (408). Adam stood resolute in the end, and
went back to Picacho. There he met an old prospector, Merryvale, who told him that Guerd Larey had been only slightly injured in the fracas fourteen years before. Thus for nought had
Adam Larey become "Wansfell the Wanderer." The twist of fate,
the strange note of irony on which the book ended, and the unresolved conflicts such as Adam's love for Ruth Virey and his
continuous search for God, suggested a sequel to *Wanderer of the
Wasteland*. When Grey wrote the sequel, he called it *Stairs of
Sand*.[17]

Wanderer of the Wasteland received much attention from
readers in this country, and pre-publication sales amounting to
over one hundred thousand copies, but, by 1923, such events
were common for a Grey work. The chief criticism of the novel
came from Burton Rascoe of the New York Tribune, who faulted
Grey for allowing Adam Larey to interfere so much in other people's affairs: "The moral ideas implicit in this book and urged
upon the readers are, in my opinion, decidedly askew."[18] Rascoe
asked: "Do Mr. Grey's readers believe in the existence of such

people as Mr. Grey depicts; do they accept the code of conduct implicit in Mr. Grey's novels?" Professor Thomas K. Whipple, who was annoyed that Grey's critics compared Grey with authors like Henry James, Jane Austen, George Eliot, and Laurence Stern, answered Rascoe in an essay for the *New York Saturday Review of Literature:*

> . . . I no more believe in the existence of such people as Mr. Grey's than I believe in the existence of the shepherds of Theocritus; I no more accept the code of conduct implicit in Mr. Grey's novels than I do the conduct implicit in Congreve's comedies . . . .
>
> . . . There is no reason for comparing him with anyone, unless perhaps with competitors in his own genre . . . . If he must be classified, however, let it be with the authors of "Beowulf" and of the Icelandic sagas. Mr. Grey's work [in its totality] is a primitive epic, and has the characteristics of other primitive epics. [19]

The sequel to *Wanderer of the Wasteland* continued the major themes inspired in Grey by the desert. *Stairs of Sand* was an appropriate title, for the book inferred that life itself is roughly comparable to "stairs of sand" that shift, change, and threaten peril. The time for *Stairs of Sand* was approximately eighteen years later than the setting in *Wanderer of the Wasteland*. Ruth Virey, a major character in *Stairs of Sand*, was Guerd's wife; she married because of pressure from her grandfather, Caleb Hunt, for he was a business partner with none other than Guerd Larey! The unhappy marriage produced in Ruth a tendency toward self-pity; indeed, Adam Larey, who had found Ruth after four years of searching, urged her to let the desert have its way with her, so she might "live to love what makes you suffer most." To endure the desert, said Adam, would make a real woman of Ruth; and allowing the desert to develop Ruth's true womanhood became the novel's major objective: "The paradox of Ruth's life was that the desert had given her many of its attributes—its changeableness, its fiery depth, its mystery and moods and passion, and its beauty; and withheld its freedom, its strength, its indifference" (253).

Stairs of Sand again asserted that the desert "seizes upon any characteristic peculiar to person or plant or animal and develops it with an appalling intensity" (23-24). At the beginning, Ruth's "peculiar," but not quite dominant, characteristic was self-pity; but, since the desert taught and intensified survival instincts, the denouement occurred when Ruth realized that she could kill Guerd Larey to prevent him from ruining several lives. This realization started Ruth on a new track: her old petulant, egotistic self vanished; she was reborn into self-reliance, and her true womanhood began to develop. Adam Larey's love for her and the desert setting taught her these things.

A sub-plot of the novel dealt with Guerd Larey's cruelty to his wife and with his plans to betray his business partner to capitalize on newly developing railroad wealth. Adam Larey was positive that Guerd's activities dictated against a long life, but who would end it? Adam had already spent fourteen years as a wanderer of the desert, expurgating his soul for a crime he did not commit. Adam was willing to kill his brother, and set out to do so, but Merryvale, the prospector, and now Adam's partner, made it unnecessary. At the novel's end, Merryvale shot Guerd twice, erasing from the desert at least one baneful influence. Adam and Ruth could now marry and live happily ever after.

IV The Changing Desert

The desert novels discussed so far were set in the late nineteenth century. The scene for *The Heritage of the Desert* was Arizona's Painted Desert; that for *Wanderer of the Wasteland* and *Stairs of Sand* the Mojave Desert of California. Implicit in the novels was a pessimistic, original-sin view of mankind. Man usually went into the desert because of some ill-fated love affair, the remembrance of which caused the desert to magnify man's baser points. If he went to find gold, he usually failed, so he spent his life on the desert brooding over his misfortunes. The desert quickly activated evil instincts in most men doomed to travel over it; and only a few people, like Adam Larey and Ruth Virey, could rise above the doleful effects of the desert.

In time, however, the desert became more habitable for the people on it. An old idea in America was that "God had hidden the New World until men were equal to its promise."[20] This concept may have motivated Grey when he wrote several novels depicting the desert as man's savior from the squalor of the East. A quickening technology—particularly in the form of the automobile—and World War I and its aftermath allowed Grey to write about a different desert from the one inhabited by Dismukes, Merryvale, and "Wansfell the Wanderer." This "new" desert had all the good and bad qualities of the "old," but the human on it had attained a technological and sociological frame of mind. Grey abhorred not only the growth of materialism caused by technology but also American involvement in world affairs. The desert, for Grey, was the great leveler; it was made livable by technology; but it taught men lessons against pervading materialism. The desert novels in this category were set in the period from 1911 to 1932, and the first one was *Desert Gold (1913)*.

V Border Strife

The setting for *Desert Gold* was the Sonora Desert along the Mexico-Arizona border, in two different time periods. The narrative began in the late nineteenth century when two men—Cameron and Warren—encountered each other in the desert. Cameron (whose real name was Burton) was in the desert to lament the loss of his wife and to punish himself by remembering her; Warren, to forget his loving daughter who had disappeared and was now presumed dead. The desert was thus to help one man to remember and another man to forget. In true Zane Grey style, the two men unknowingly were father-in-law and son-in-law to each other, for the missing woman turned out to be young Cameron's lost wife, and the aged Warren's lost daughter! The two men became lost in the desert. Warren soon died. Before Cameron expired, he found a fabulous treasure of gold. He marked the place for someone's future reference and with the certificate proving his marriage to Nell Warren.

Desert Gold then shifted to the early part of the twentieth century, about the year 1911. A revolution was raging in Mexico, producing troublous times for American settlements in the vicinity. Some of the Mexican riders were not revolutionists at all, but bandits who crossed the international border at will. One such person was Rojas, the kidnaper of a beautiful maiden, Mercedes Castaneda. Mercedes' lover, George Thorpe, enlisted the aid of Richard Gale (a rich Easterner in the West to prove his manhood) to wrest Mercedes from Rojas' grasp. Richard caused a commotion to divert Rojas' attention; and, during the turmoil, he escaped with Mercedes. He received help in this endeavor from two cowboys, Ladd and Lash, who guided the fugitives to the ranch of Belding, United States Inspector of Immigration. Belding had a step-daughter named Nell Burton.

At Belding's ranch, Richard got a job patrolling the border to prevent illegal entry. On patrol one day Richard came to a waterhole. Mexican bandits were encamped there, so Richard watched them from a safe distance. Two Indians happened upon the scene, one a Papago, the other a Yaqui.[21] The Mexicans killed the Papago and then tried to stamp the Yaqui to death with their horses. At this point, Richard drove off the Mexicans and rescued the Indian. Soon afterward Richard learned of the irrepressible hatred between Mexicans and Yaquis. The Mexicans enslaved the Yaquis (Mountain Aztecs) and set them to work in the henequin fields of the Yucatan Peninsula. When Richard's Yaqui survived, he became Richard's teacher: " . . . [A]lways before him was an example that made him despair of a white man's equality, color, race, blood, breeding—what were these in the wilderness?" Through Yaqui, the desert taught Richard tenaciousness of life, stoicism, and endurance of strength: a far cry from the free-wheeling life he had pursued in the East.

Rojas appeared at the ranch to recapture Mercedes. To escape him, Richard, Thorpe, Mercedes, and the two cowboys, Ladd and Lash, started a long trip to Yuma across treacherous lava beds. Without the primitive abilities of Yaqui, the group would have perished. Rojas followed, but was tricked by Yaqui, and plunged down a cliff to his death. The group remained in the lava fields for several weeks while Ladd recuperated from bullet wounds and from having a choya cactus blade driven into his face while fighting Rojas.

When the group returned to Belding's ranch, many changes had transpired. A land promoter, Ben Chase, had all but cheated Belding out of his holdings; and his son, Radford, had become another "Rojas" in relation to Nell. Also, Richard's parents, who had come from the East to visit their prodigal son, were amazed to hear of his exploits, and were astounded that their son, who came from a wealthy family, worked for forty dollars a month. It did not take long for Richard Gale to set things aright after his return: he beat Radford Chase to a pulp and forced Ben Chase to stop harassing Belding. This revenge did not bring back Belding's property, however, nor did it erase the fact that Chase had staked legitimate claims to most of the remaining land in the area.

At this dark point, Yaqui bade Richard to follow him into the No-Name Mountains. Going to the source of the Forlorn River, they found the gold which Burton (Cameron) had left many years before. They also discovered a twenty-one-year-old certificate which recorded the marriage of Burton and Nell Warren, the present Mrs. Belding. This proved that Nell Burton was not illegitimate, and destroyed the last obstacle to her marriage to Richard. On the day of the wedding, Yaqui went home—to the lava beds. His work was done, for he had fashioned Richard Gale into a powerful force.

Grey used the same basic themes in *Desert Gold* as he had in his other novels: individualism, edenic and healing qualities of the West, and the transforming power of the desert. The author, however, developed two new thoughts in *Desert Gold*; and one of these was the role of the heroine. Rojas constantly told Mercedes that he would reform if she would love him. When she refused, Rojas became meaner than ever; and he blamed Mercedes for the deterioration. Radford Chase played the same game with Nell Burton: if Nell would return his love, he would become a model citizen. If she would not, said Radford, she would cause him to do things, the responsibility for which he could not accept. Grey presented this dilemma to many of his heroines, and in one novel he allowed the heroine to give the love that the bad man wanted; but, since it was to no avail, he indicated that appeasement of evil-doers was a mistake.

The second new development in *Desert Gold* was anti-racism, for Grey portrayed the tragic aspects of racial hatred. Not only in *Desert Gold*, but in a short story titled "Yaqui," Grey wrote of the internecine strife between the Mexicans and the Yaquis. The Yaquis had lived for centuries in the Sierra Madres, and like the United States Indians, they were unsettled by gold prospectors. They moved from the mountains into the desert, and finally they went to the lava beds from which could be seen in the distance the Gulf of California. Even in this forlorn place, the Yaquis were not safe; for each winter the gold-seekers came from the South. The animosities generated between the Yaquis and Mexicans amounted to a war of extermination in which time dictated against the Indians. Grey's sympathy for American Indians who were mistreated by white settlers was well known; and his support of the Yaquis against the Mexicans harmonized perfectly with his oft-stated views.

The continuing strife along the Mexican border prompted another desert novel, *The Light of Western Stars* (1914). When Madeline ("Majesty") Hammond, a New York society girl, bought a ranch in Southern Arizona, the operation of it became involved in the struggle between Mexican leaders Francisco Madero and Victoriano Huerta. Majesty's favorite cowboy, Gene Stewart (called El Capitan), joined the Madero faction and fought against Don Carlos, a wealthy Mexican supporter of Huerta. The belligerency between these two moved the novel's events along at a rapid pace.

A highlight in the novel was "cowboy golf." President William Howard Taft popularized golf in the United States, so it was natural for Grey to feature the game in one of his books. The cowboys were entranced by golf, begging off work to practice. When some of Majesty's Eastern friends visited the ranch, a golf "tournament" was arranged. The event proceeded nicely until Monty Price disagreed with the umpire, an Englishman named Castleton, about the lay of the ball. Monty discussed the matter with his hand on his six-shooter, a fact that considerably tempered Castleton's rebuttal. The "tournament" ended amid merrymaking from the spectators.

In addition to golf, the automobile was a feature in *The Light of Western Stars*. The old time cowboys distrusted the car, saying it would never take the place of the horse and buggy. Even Link Stevens, the "chauffeur," thought he was breaking a bronc when he drove the vehicle. He could travel sixty-three miles in an hour and fifteen minutes. Understandably, other occupants of the car were usually reluctant passengers.

If it had not been for the automobile, Gene Stewart would have been executed by the Mexican revolutionists. Captured by them, he was sentenced to death; but "Majesty" used her wealth and power to contact prominent Senators in Washington who interceded on Stewart's behalf and got him pardoned. Though Stewart was pardoned, the site of the execution was Mezquital, well over a hundred miles from "Majesty's" Ranch and cut off from telegraphic facilities. The only way to get word to the officials in time to stop the killing was a wild automobile ride in which Stevens made record time despite several blow-outs caused by choya. Because the party got to Mezquital just in time to save Gene, he and "Majesty" respected automobiles for the rest of their lives.

In time, after their marriage, "Majesty" bore Stewart a child. They named her Madge and called her "Majesty." Her career as a young college lady encouraged Grey to write a sequel to *The Light of Western Stars*, the novel *Majesty's Rancho*.

As Grey's novels appeared more and more rapidly, the story spread that he never revised after he had finished writing. Several reviews and essays reported that after he gave his manuscript to Dolly, he never looked at it again until it was in print. Grey did, however, edit *The Light of Western Stars* and some of his other novels. He wrote Murphy in July, 1912:

Dear Dan,

Dolly agrees with you about the detached nature of several of these chapters. I "sit" on myself too much to please Mr. H[arper's?] and a lot of critics.

I must go back, cut out, condense, change a little, and write in more story & action.

My idea is to bring forth Pat Hawe [a sheriff in the novel who was badge happy] & Don Carlos, and make a strong scene *before* the cowboy golf chapter.

Then I'll improve that. I'll write in some more action, etc., just after that chapter. Then I'll cut the "Mountain Trail," the Crags" a little to help along with the idea.

What do you think of this?

The succeding chapters according to Dolly *are splendid*.

Got my statement from Harpers. 20000 copies of Riders [of the Purple Sage] sold before the last edition! Isn't that fine?

Let me have a line from you.

Sincerely,

Zane[22]

By the time Grey wrote *Majesty's Rancho* (1937), the internal combustion engine was in ill-repute with many lovers of old-fashioned ways; for the setting in time of the plot was the mid 1930's. Gene Stewart, now an aging man and doting father, was bothered by cattle rustling. He and his men could not understand why the cattle tracks ended at the state highway until the book's hero, Lance Sidway, deduced correctly that the stolen cattle were hauled away in trucks. Rustling had become a mechanical art, and the gangster elements, led by "Honey Bee" Uhl, invaded the territory with their big gaudy cars and their slick methods of operation. "Progress" in the form of motorized vehicles exacted a high price from society in the changed lives it brought about.

"Majesty," now a college student, typified much of the changed thinking among young people. As she told her mother: "For young people [the] modern thing seems to be to break all the laws—speed laws, booze laws! There is no such thing as modesty, as I remember you taught it to me. Pagans, I fear! I haven't opened a Bible since my religion course during my sophomore year" (109). "Majesty" finally saw the light and changed her ways because of Lance Sidway's love and because of the deep influence of the desert around her. But thousands of other young people did not change; and Grey talked about them in a novel, *The Call of the Canyon*.

VI   The Lure of the Desert

In *The Call of the Canyon* (1924) Carley Burke went to the West to find Glenn Kilbourne, her fiancé, who had left the East to recuperate from wounds received in World War I. She found him, but he would not return to New York with her; he preferred the life of a hog farmer to that of a businessman. Finally, Carley left without him, but not before buying some land in the Arizona desert. Returned to New York City, Carley constantly compared life in the East and West, and frequently found herself on the defensive about the West. Her friend Eleanor stated the modernist's viewpoint: "The preachers and reformers and bishops and rabbis make me sick. They rave about jazz. Jazz—the discordant note of our decadence.—The idiots! If they could be women for a while they would realize the errors of their ways. But they will never, never abolish jazz—*never*, for it is the grandest, the most wonderful, the most absolutely necessary thing for women in this terrible age of smotheration" (234). Finally, Carley could sustain no more of such talk, so she uttered a dreadful malediction on her associates and their way of life. What was wrong with this country? Carley Burke told them.

The role of women was especially despicable to Carley: women got the vote, only to stay away from the polls; women mocked prohibition laws; and they allowed their children to go to dance halls and movie theaters. Young girls aped the women by wearing short skirts, using lipstick, and plucking their eyebrows. Women actually stood on street corners distributing pamphlets urging birth control. Women could not stand childbirth; or, if they did, they would not nurse their babies themselves. Carley closed her tirade with these words: "You doll women, you parasites, you toys of men, you silken-wrapped geisha girls, you painted, idle, purring cats, you parody of the females of your species—find brains enough if you can to see the doom hanging over you and revolt before it is too late!" (247). In rejection of urban life, Carley hastened back to her canyons to marry Glenn Kilbourne.

For anyone who wondered about the source of Grey's popularity, Carley's condemnation of urban life and values gave them the answer. Grey's audience, the middle-and lower-middle class had value judgments essentially rural; and they applauded when someone spoke as harshly to the city element as Carley Burke did. Most of Grey's work was serialized in magazines appealing to middle-class standards; *Call of the Canyon*, for example, appeared in *Ladies' Home Journal* in several installments in 1921 and 1922. Among the other magazines that frequently serialized Grey's novels were *The Country Gentleman* and *Collier's Weekly*.

L. H. Robbins, reviewing the book in the *New York Times*, credited Grey's appeal in part to the cleanness and freshness of his stories: "Is it possible that even now [1924] the majority of readers like their fiction decent? Is it possible that the Sophisticates, with all their ballyhooing for this candid novel or that pathologic play, have not yet prevailed against the standards of respectability that seems to them so deplorable?"[23] Robbins complimented *The Call of the Canyon* for its understanding of sex [presumably by his treatment of sex in an inoffensive manner]: "Mr. Grey demonstrates that one may touch Freud without being defiled." The scenery in the novel "does more than fill space. Potent in its influence upon the people of the story, it is a character in itself; the leading character indeed. The wild, lonely, fearfully beautiful Arizona desert has never been better done."[24]

Grey's attacks against post-World War I standards were so appealing that he continued writing novels, articles, and short stories on the subject. One of his most cutting assaults on the "new morality" came in *The Day of the Beast* an Eastern novel. Not dealing with the desert, it maintained, nevertheless, the theme of lamentation over the condition to which America had degenerated. The book was serialized in 1922 in *The Country Gentleman*.[25] Other books emphasizing this theme and using the desert as a cure for evil were *Captives of the Desert*, serialized as *Desert Bound* in 1925 by *McCall's* and *The Lost Pueblo*. The latter was published in 1927 by *Collier's Weekly* under the title of *The Water-Hole*.

Grey believed that the novelist has "an appalling responsibility in these modern days of materialism to dare to foster idealism and love of nature, chivalry in men and chastity in women."[26] In fulfilling his role as a social force, Grey became highly moralistic. A book like *The Call of the Canyon* may have struck reviewer Robbins as "clean and fresh" due, in part, to the absence of violent death in its pages; and such an absence was a rarity since only a few of Grey's books avoided violence. Most were replete with sudden, awful death; the casualty rate climbed sometimes into the hundreds within the space of three hundred or so pages. These somber events occurred in a setting that was both beautiful and deadly: the desert. If a man's good qualities were ascendant, the desert developed them; if his bad qualities were predominant (as in the case of most people), the desert promoted them and made their possessor little short of a beast. Grey illustrated this point endlessly in such novels as *Wanderer of the Wasteland*, *Stairs of Sand*, and *Black Mesa* (published in 1955).

When one considered these possibilities of the desert in developing man's good or bad traits, the picture of the urban East became forlorn indeed—enough so to cause millions of readers to yearn for Western parts. Since most people were unable to go West, they went vicariously with Zane Grey. He was their guide, and in the process, he became much more influential than historian Frederick Jackson Turner in interpreting the value of the West—both historically and contemporarily—to the American public. The desert caused Grey to explore the themes of survival of the fittest and to contrast new trends with old. In pursuing this course, many of his novels in this category were alike, with Grey adopting a "preaching" stance. The criticism was sometimes made that Grey only wrote one novel, for everything else was just a variant. This criticism was valid only in part for categories of Grey's writing, such as deserts, mountains and cowboys, and was not valid at all for his work as a whole.

The desert was first in Grey's affections for places because it brought out the "ineradicable and unconscious wildness of savage nature in man," and tested him in respect to character and fortitude. He used the desert to show men away from civilization pitted against nature in much the same way as Joseph Conrad used the sea. It was to the barren wastelands that a man must go to transcend mere existence, to find his soul, and to grasp the idea of what Charles Darwin called "natural selection." After the desert, the mountains intrigued Grey; they complemented the desert by showing that nature was larger than human life, causing the pensive man to ponder his origins and his fate. Within this reflective framework came the knowledge of evolution of all living things and the significance of the balance of nature. Grey thoroughly explored these themes in his work categorized as "Mountain Novels."

CHAPTER 3

The Mountain Novels

A deeply ingrained love of nature inspired Zane Grey to write, and the fields and streams of Zanesville and Lackawaxen first taught him this love. His trip West with "Buffalo" Jones in 1907 nurtured it, and his note-taking excursions into the deserts and mountains matured it. After 1910, he was increasingly absent from his home in Lackawaxen and from the residence which he maintained in Middlebury, New York. He spent his time in the Western regions, practicing the art of "silent watching." At the same time, Grey became enamored of the evolutionary theories of Charles Darwin. These influences on Grey within a mountain setting added to what Jim Emett had already taught him, and helped Grey to write some of his most memorable novels.

His sense of history was enlarged by coming into contact with several Mormons in mountainous surroundings. He became much interested in Mormonism—what it had been and what it was becoming. Personally, he did not like Mormons because, in his opinion, they mistreated women and were religious fanatics.[1] Grey's disdainful attitude toward Mormonism as an institution was implied in *The Heritage of the Desert* (1910). Two years later, when *Riders of the Purple Sage* was printed, his anti-Mormonism was complete. In this book, generally acknowledged as his most popular, Grey elaborated upon the price one must pay to retain personal beliefs; and he showed the tragedy in human lives when a group refused to believe that "good" and "bad" are relative terms.

I Riders of the Purple Sage (1912)

Mormonism in its ugliest form was delineated in *Riders of the Purple Sage*. Jane Withersteen, heiress of a fortune left by her Mormon father, befriended Berne Venters, non-Mormon. Mormon Elder Tull and his associates, who took exception to this treatment, prepared to whip Venters; but, at the critical moment, Lassiter, a well-known gunman, arrived and rescued Venters. Extreme hatred existed between Lassiter and the Mormons; for Lassiter had been searching eighteen years for his sister, Millie Erne, who had been lured away from her husband by Mormons. In retaliation, the Mormons blinded Lassiter's horse by roping it and holding hot irons near its eyes. They swore to kill Lassiter; but, since the former Texan was a "fast-draw" with his six-shooters, the Mormons were wary. When Lassiter discovered that Milly was dead, he set out to find the Mormon who had ruined her life; therefore, the theme of revenge was firmly established at the novel's beginning. Jane Withersteen tried to dissuade Lassiter, telling him that vengeance did not belong to man, but to God. Jane's trial, then, was to keep Lassiter from killing again (because it was implicit, though not stated, that she loved him) and to reconcile herself to harassment for befriending non-Mormons while retaining her Mormonism.

The Mormons of Cottonwood, the village where Jane lived in 1871, did not exactly pursue a "reign of terror" against non-Mormons or those Mormons who cooperated with them. But Elder Tull (who wanted Jane for one of his wives), Bishop Dyer, and their followers made life uncomfortable for anyone departing from the rigid codes of uniformity inculcated by the Mormon Church. They stampeded Jane's cattle by waving white flags, by using a mirror to deflect the rays of the sun into the cattle's faces, and by setting a coyote's tail afire and turning the animal loose amid the herd. The Mormon leaders were especially incensed when Jane took in a non-Mormon girl whose mother had died; and little Fay Larkin became a central figure in Grey's later book, *The Rainbow Trail*.

As time passed, Jane's dilemma worsened. She hired Lassiter to ride for her, yet wanted him to throw away his guns. Lassiter hotly refused: "Gun-packing in the West since the Civil War has growed into a kind of moral law" (132). Although the Mormon leadership intensified its drive by turning Jane's house servants against her and by stealing her prize horses, she still would not renounce the faith in which she was reared. Lassiter simply could not understand Jane's position: "Among many thousands of women you're one who has bucked against your churchmen. They tried you out, an' failed of persuasion, an' finally of threats—you meet now the cold steel of a will as far from Christlike as the universe is wide. What do they care for your soul?" (146).

While Jane and Lassiter confronted the Mormons of Cottonwood, Venters, riding for Jane, had an adventure of his own when he was accosted by an outlaw, Oldring, and a "masked rider." Venters shot the "masked rider," only to discover that "he" was a girl named Bess. For several weeks Venters nursed the gunshot victim, fervently praying that she would not die. When she was well enough to move, Venters headed back for Cottonwood; but on the way he found a secluded valley, the entrance of which was guarded by a great balancing rock, put there no doubt by ancient peoples to ward off enemy attacks. If the rock ever rolled, Surprise Valley, as Venters called his and Bess's paradise, would be isolated from the world.

Long after Bess's complete recovery, the two made no effort to leave: they found numerous signs of a primitive life that once had flourished in the valley; they found food supplies; they found gold; and, naturally, they found their love for each other. The valley caused the two lovers to ponder the meaning of existence: Bess asked, "Did the people who lived here once have the same feelings as we have? What was the good of their living at all? They're gone! What's the meaning of it all—of us?" Venters replied, "Maybe we're higher in the scale of human beings—in intelligence. But who knows? We can't be any higher in the things for which life is lived at all."

"What are they?"
"Why—I suppose relationship, friendship, love."
"Love!"
"Yes, love of man for woman—love of woman for man. That's the nature, the meaning, the best of life itself" (152).

Thus, love between one man and one woman was the noblest function of mankind. This thought came close to being a major theme not only in *Riders of the Purple Sage* but in several other Grey novels.

Venters occasionally left his valley for grain and vegetables, neither of which was in great supply. On one such trip, Lassiter secretly trailed Venters, learned of Surprise Valley, but did not tell Jane of his discovery. Events rapidly came to a head at Cottonwood as Lassiter, positive that it was Bishop Dyer who had led his sister Millie Erne astray, swore to kill him for all the misery he had caused. Jane entreated Lassiter to forget his revenge, but not even Jane's admission that it was her own father who had defiled Lassiter's sister altered his decision. Lassiter exterminated Dyer by first shooting him in the arms and then methodically pumping bullets into his body. After the deed, Lassiter and Jane fled from an enraged Mormon citizenry.

Lassiter headed for Surprise Valley, in the vicinity of which he met Venters and Bess, who were leaving for Venters' old home in Quincy, Illinois. When Jane learned that Venters and Bess had lived together in Surprise Valley for several weeks, she was infuriated. Despite her Mormonism which, as she had often said, nullified the possibility of any amorous attachment to Venters or to any other non-Mormon, Jane felt slighted and suffered a twinge of jealousy. She expressed her feelings, though she and Lassiter were being pursued by Elder Tull and the Mormons. All became well, however, when Lassiter told Bess's story as he had heard it from Oldring: Bess was really Elizabeth Erne, daughter of Millie. Bishop Dyer had stolen Elizabeth from Millie when Elizabeth was three years old, and he had given her to Oldring to be raised as an outlaw, an action undertaken to destroy any chance that Elizabeth's real parents would regain her. Though an outlaw, Oldring loved Bess as a daughter and developed her character in positive, humanitarian ways. Lassiter's revelation mollified Jane, and she gave Venters and Bess her two favorite horses, Night and Black Star, to facilitate their flight from Utah.

On the trail again, Lassiter, Jane, and Fay Larkin managed to get to the opening of Surprise Valley. While Lassiter fought off the Mormon pursuers, "phases of the history of the world flashed through [Jane's] mind—Greek and Roman wars, dark, mediaeval times, the crimes in the name of religion. Greed, power, oppression, fanaticism, love, hate, revenge, justice, freedom—for these, men killed one another" (273). Just before Tull and his men surrounded the besieged couple and child, Lassiter rolled the balancing rock, closing the outlet to Surprise Valley. He wavered at the start, but Jane shouted her love to him above the din of gun-fire, and without hesitation, he heaved the rock into place. They stayed in Surprise Valley for many years until a young preacher from Illinois, disheartened by the narrow beliefs of his Protestant congregation, came West at the bidding of Venters and Bess, who had long ago married, and found them. The minister's name was John Shefford, and Grey told his story in *The Rainbow Trail*, the sequel to *Riders of the Purple Sage*.

In *Riders of the Purple Sage*, Grey developed two themes traditionally common to the West, and one that was universal in application. The role of the frontier woman was the first, the necessity of the "fast-draw" artist to the growth of the West was next, and third was the strong appeal for relativism in matters of moral judgment.

Jane Withersteen could have led a very comfortable life, honored by her fellow churchmen. Since she chose, however, to help people other than those inured to Mormondom, she was harassed and even terrorized. Jane personified the frontier woman: courageous, determined, changeable, indispensable. Grey did not say why Jane differed so much from the religion of her father and the other Mormon officials. Apparently Jane did not personally believe she had betrayed Mormonism—she made references to retaining her religion; on the contrary, she thought Mormonism had forsaken her. She did not approve an intolerant treatment of her fellowmen. She saw the necessity of change to which other Mormons were blind; thus, like August Naab in Grey's earlier novel, Jane Withersteen was symbolic of a changing institution, the Mormon Church.

Sharply different from Jane's ways—which in themselves were vital to Western development—was the gunman. Throughout the book Grey constantly drew contrasts between the gentle callings of Jane and the violent missions of Lassiter, but at the end he made it quite clear that both conditions were of equal importance in settling the West. Not only in *Riders of the Purple Sage*, but in dozens of other novels, Grey wrote of the gunman. Generally a gunman was a cowboy wronged either by a woman or the law. He did not usually like to kill—Grey's fast-drawer was sickened each time he shot a man—but, when he had established a reputation, he had to protect it in every little town he visited. Luckily, the inclinations of most gunmen were toward law and order. Without their help, ordinary men simply could not have coped with the lawless elements. Grey was thus complimentary of most of the gunmen he discussed in the thousands of pages he wrote.

The third major theme in *Riders* was the relativism of moral persuasions: there was much evil in Bishop Dyer, a man who presented to the world a visage of benevolence; but there was much good in Oldring, known to the outside world as a vicious outlaw. The Christian ethic could be stated in different ways by different people, and still be legitimate: a man's calling or his religion were not necessarily an index to his ideas of humanity. (Grey demonstrated this especially well in some of his Indian novels.) In this connection, Grey showed that of all fanaticisms, religious fanaticism was the worst because it stripped its victim of any self-pride or identification. Religious intolerance also caused a great deal of unnecessary conflict and bloodshed. Grey applied the dictum "You must change to stay where you are" to Mormonism.

Failure to reform and fanaticism hastened the radical changes that ultimately affected the Mormon Church.

That the reading public enthusiastically accepted *Riders of the Purple Sage* was indicated by huge sales of the book and by favorable reviews. The *Review of Reviews* liked *Riders of the Purple Sage* because it was not servile to any European model but was pure Americana, though exaggerated fiction: "The ruthlessness of Mormonism in that period of Western development is laid bare with great accuracy and the literary artistry of the book is superior to that of many that have been praised above it."[2] *The Nation* computed the mortality rate in the book at well over a hundred, caused primarily by Lassiter and Venters in their efforts to escape the revenge of Mormondom. The story contained all the emotional elements, said the *Nation*, that had ever been dreamed of or invented.[3] Even the New York *Times* was kind to Grey on this occasion; its reviewer lauded *Riders of the Purple Sage* as superior to Grey's earlier book, *The Heritage of the Desert*. *Riders* was closer knit in construction, better balanced in component elements, and more poignant in its emotional qualities.[4] Further evidence of the book's popularity was the proposal by a Mr. Van Brunt in 1913 that he dramatize the story for stage production—a suggestion never fulfilled, though some of Grey's later works were turned into plays.[5] As late as 1950, the American State Department wanted to translate *Riders* into Annamese for propaganda purposes in Indo-China, but this plan did not materialize.[6]

II   *The Rainbow Trail* (1915)

Even before *Riders* was published, Grey was busily working on another novel about the American West, *The Rainbow Trail*, which dealt with the Reverend John Shefford, who went to the West from Quincy, Illinois, in part to forget the quarrels with his congregation, and also to find Cottonwoods, where Jane Withersteen, Lassiter, and Fay Larkin had lived. Cottonwoods, however, was now abandoned, and in its place were several "sealed wife" villages, such as Stonebridge, in which Mormons hid their wives to escape prosecution by the federal government for practicing polygamy. While in Stonebridge, Shefford attended a Mormon service; and he concluded that both Mormon and other religions suffered from the same weakness: they existed only to uphold the founders of a church. He asked, "is there no religion divorced from power?"

In the Mormon village was a mysterious woman named Mary,

called the Sago Lily; and Shefford wondered if Mary were one of the sealed wives. He started meeting her frequently, and he learned in due time that the Sago Lily was none other than Fay Larkin! (Grey never explained how or when Fay had left Surprise Valley.) She was not a sealed wife, nor even a Mormon, although the Mormon community exerted great pressure upon her to join them. In a way, she relived the experiences of Jane Withersteen of an earlier age. Finally in desperation, Fay and Shefford fled from Stonebridge to escape the Mormons who were tormenting her and from the glare of publicity caused by government investigations into the sealed-wife villages.

The two headed for Surprise Valley by the path Fay had memorized. There they found Jane Withersteen and Jim Lassiter who had lived for many years in the secluded Paradise. When the group left, and headed for Nonnezoshe, "the Rainbow Bridge,"[7] it was guided by a Navajo, Nas Ta Bega, and followed by an Indian renegade, Shadd. They finally eluded their pursuers, got to a trading post, and made plans to go to Illinois, where Berne and Bess Venters were waiting to see them.

The Rainbow Trail was serialized as *The Desert Crucible* in 1915 by *Argosy*. The book's main thrust was the continuing change in Mormonism in the last quarter of the nineteenth century; for a young generation of Mormons was more willing to change than its elders had been. Historical themes dealt with sealed-wife villages and the conflict between the government and long-established religious habits. Themes of religious prejudice, with the intent of showing that there was little difference between Mormon and non-Mormon narrowness, ran throughout the book. And, finally, Grey continued a theme that he had emphasized in previous books: the mistreatment of Indians by the white man. Both Nas Ta Bega (who actually existed) and Shadd were wronged, but each reacted differently: Nas Ta Bega used his powers for good; Shadd, for evil.

Grey was pleased with *The Rainbow Trail*, and well he might have been. Mary Roberts Rinehart wrote a glowing review of it, former skeptic Ripley Hitchcock sent a warm letter of congratulations, and Dolly Grey spoke of it as one of her husband's "thinking novels."[8] Before too many more years passed, Grey was publicly heralded as the writer most in demand by publishers; and Harper's offered first a five- and then a ten-year contract. In the midst of his growing popularity as a literary authority, Grey tried to keep things in perspective: to write every day (though he did not always do this), to fish whenever possible, and to avoid morbid spells of depression. History, cowboys, and horseflesh continued to fascinate him; but he always turned to the mountains for the real lessons of nature.

III   Darwinian Influences

Grey's 1920 novel, *Man of the Forest*, showed more clearly than most of his books how moutainous settings inspired thoughts of evolution; but the story itself was typical of Grey. Milt Dale was regarded by the citizens of Pine, Arizona, as lazy and shiftless because he would not take a job on a ranch. Milt was gifted as a mechanic, however, so the people of Pine were always happy to see him. When Helen Rayner and her sister Bo came to Pine from the East to oversee their ailing uncle's ranch, Grey gave a preview of the novel's theme as Milt told Helen that actually to know the value of life, one must do five things at one time or another; go hungry, be away from home, face death, desire to kill someone, and be madly in love. The book's plot involved Helen's apprenticeship as a rancher, evil men's trying to take her property, and Milt's foiling their designs. The love affair between Milt and Helen was easily predictable.

The novel was replete with passages about the evolution of man from a state of barbarism to that of civilization. Such statements indicated that man was but a part of a grand, inscrutable design in which the trials of life such as Milt had mentioned were necessary to all living things. Put into other terms, the statements amounted to thoughts of "natural selection," or "survival of the fittest." Charles Darwin said in *The Descent of Man*: "Natural selection follows from the struggle for existence; and this from a rapid rate of increase."[9] Zane Grey said in *Man of the Forest*: "If you're quick to see, you'll learn that the nature here in the wilds is the same as that of men—trees fight to live—birds fight—animals fight—men fight. They all live off one another" (126).

When Darwinists made these points in the early part of the twentieth century, the rural and small-town middle classes usually charged them with error about human nature or with atheism. Yet when Zane Grey said the same things in less formal language the middle classes regarded him as a man of great common sense and insight. Thus, Grey unwittingly became an acceptable interpreter of Darwinism to a great mass of America's citizens; and the impact was significant. It was not only in *Man of the Forest* that these thoughts were evident but also in several other novels.

Lucy Watson, for example, in *Under the Tonto Rim* (1926), thought: "In ages back all the wandering tribes of men had to hunt to live, and their problems were few . . . . [T]hrough the long ages, these savages had progressed mentally and spiritually. Lucy saw that as a law of life" (80). This novel concerned a female social worker who went into the wild Tonto Country of central Arizona to work with the settlers. At first Lucy believed she symbolized the advanced culture of her day: "These backwoods people were many generations behind city people in their development" (80). At the end of the book, however, Lucy Watson, social worker, married Edd Denmeade, hunter of wild bees and a resident of the Tonto. Grey was a close student of Darwin, so evolutionary beliefs in his novels were to be expected. Moreover, Grey wrote most of the books dealing with this subject in a remote mountain fastness in the shadow of the Tonto Rim where he had an excellent chance to study nature first hand, to read Darwin, and to incorporate these points into his written work. *Under the Tonto Rim* first appeared in 1925 in the pages of *Ladies' Home Journal*.[10] Its original title was *The Bee Hunter*, but it was changed, partly because Gene Stratton Porter's new novel, *Keeper of the Bees*, could conceivably cause confusion.[11] *Man of the Forest* was serialized in 1917 by *The Country Gentleman*. Though Grey found it difficult to concentrate on revising the novel for book publication, it proved to be one of his most popular efforts. Related in principle to *Man of the Forest* was *The Deer Stalker*, a 1925 serialization in *The Country Gentlemen* which was published in book form in 1949. The deer population on Buckskin Mountain in northern Arizona had increased because of unrestrained slaughter of cougars. When the deer multiplied so fast that there were not enough grazes and forages for them, they faced starvation. The balance of nature had been broken, said one of the characters in the book: "Herds of deer, running free, will never thrive whar' the cougars have been killed off. The price of healthy life in the open is eternal vigilance— eternal watch an' struggle against death by violence. Man cain't remove the balance an' expect Nature to correct it. These heah ain't had nothin' to check their overbreedin' and inbreedin'. They jest doubled and trebled" (16).

The government's "solution" to the problem caused anguish among the forest rangers of Buckskin Mountain, for unhampered hunting designed to destroy twenty-five thousand deer was decided upon. Thad Eberne, the chief ranger, was ultimately dismissed from the forestry service for objecting to hundreds of unskilled hunters who had invaded the area and in many instances had not killed the deer but had inflicted painful injuries upon them. Rangers spent days following the path of hunters to find the results of their amateurism and to kill the wounded, crippled deer. The whole gory situation illustrated to Grey the baneful effects of man's meddling with nature.

This preoccupation with nature, its balance, its beauty, and its evolution dominated the Grey novels about the wild, mountainous regions of the Tonto Country. One such novel, *Stranger from the Tonto*, (1956) was a contrived story. Its hero, Kent Wingfield, made most of his decisions about love and action before he had ever met the other characters. His mountain heritage, though, was the most significant thing about Wingfield; as in so many of his novels, Grey made setting and description more important than characterization.

When Wingfield set out to rescue a girl, Lucy Bonesteel, from Southern Utah's notorious Hole in the Wall Gang, he developed his instincts for survival and his sense of nature matured in doing so. In Utah, Wingfield stood in awe of the canyon country: "He felt the awful solemnity of the eons that had produced this phenomenon, the august reign of a spirit to which time, life, death were nothing, the invisible proof of eternity" (213). Wingfield not only saved Lucy but also rehabilitated her father, Avid Bonesteel, the leader of the Hole in the Wall Gang. This effort succeeded because of Wingfield's superior background. Grey once more endowed a character with super-human qualities, thereby causing doubts among the critics of his sense of realism.

The same thing occurred in another of Grey's mountain novels, *The Mysterious Rider*, serialized in *The Country Gentleman*, published as a book in 1921, and turned into a play in 1923, called *Hell-Bent Wade*. Set in the late nineteenth century in Colorado, the novel concerned the love of a man for his spoiled son. Bill Bellounds simply could not grasp what everybody else saw, that his son Jack was a thoroughly rotten person. Bill even expected Columbine, whom he had reared after rescuing her from Indians, to become Jack's bride. Columbine's lot, as well as that of her cowboy sweetheart, Wilson Moore, was desperate until a mysterious rider appeared known as "Hell-Bent" Wade because of the bad luck that always seemed to follow him.

Wade had wrongly accused his wife of infidelity eighteen years before; and, as a result, she had left his house, taking their young daughter with her. Indians had killed the mother, and had apparently kidnapped the daughter. So "Hell-Bent" became a wanderer, doomed to a life of self-punishment because of his base deed. As had Adam Larey in *Wanderer of the Wasteland*, Wade deliberately sought situations in which he could be of service to his fellow human beings; for through good works, he believed he could atone for his past sins. It was only natural, then, for Wade to be interested in a doting father who was trying to marry his horrible son to his lovely adopted daughter. When Wade took employment at the Bellound's Ranch and was soon in the midst of events, he made efforts to reform Jack Bellounds, but in vain. Finally, when Wade discovered that Jack was rustling his own father's cattle and laying the deed to Wilson Moore, he decided to rid the world of a problem. He and Jack shot it out, both becoming casualties. While this occurred, Columbine discovered that Wade was her father. The story ended with Columbine and Wilson planning their marriage.

The Mysterious Rider was a study of the loner, so familiar to students of Western history. There was a direct line between "Wansfell the Wanderer" and "Hell-Bent" Wade. Each, in his own way, fought the elements, but mostly himself. In the process, each contributed greatly to the betterment of the human race; and they were proof that, through suffering and struggle, there was "survival of the fittest." There were many loners in Grey's treatment of the West, but these two were the most typical. Grey was eminently qualified to write about loners, for he was largely one himself, at least concerning literature; for he disliked most of the literary forms of his day. He once visited a publisher and was given an advertisement of a national, best-selling novel as an example of what his own writing should be. Grey hated the novel in question, for "it is as far from literature as the world is wide." Grey told the publisher that he would be ashamed to have his name on such a book.[12] Thus, Grey very definitely set himself apart from most literature of the time. It seemed only natural for several of his novels to deal with individuals who ran counter to prevailing trends.

The play produced from *The Mysterious Rider* contained four acts and was done in collaboration with a New York dramatist, Frank McGlynn.[13] Though the play tended to be even more melodramatic than the novel, it did stress the nature of life, its brevity, and its cruelty. A major weakness of the play was that a main incident—one involving Jack's fight with Wilson and one that inspired much of the subsequent action—took place completely off stage. Thus, the audience (if there ever was one, for there is no evidence that this play was performed) had to guess many of the play's motivating factors. In the book, Wade and Jack killed each other; in the play, however, Bill Bellounds finally learned the truth about his son and banished him. At that same time, "Hell-Bent" Wade departed to continue his life's mission of helping people. The curtain fell as Columbine rushed to Wade, calling him "Father!"

Happily for his supporters and for the literary world at large, Grey did not try to write too many plays. His great strength was in novels and short stories, and to these he committed himself. His mountain novels continued to emphasize the themes of evolution, of survival of the fittest, of the beauty of Nature, and of the loner. *Sunset Pass*, (1931) set in New Mexico, and *Robber's Roost*, (1932) in the mountains of Southern Utah, presented additional discussions of the loner. In *Sunset Pass*, Trueman Rock operated out of Wagontongue, New Mexico, to find a man and his sons who rustled cattle, killed them, and sold the meat. Rock's chief dilemma was that he fell in love with the culprit's daughter; but as in so many other of Grey's novels, the hero not only won the hand of the maiden but reformed through love and example the erring parents. *Robber's Roost* was about outlaws who captured a beautiful woman, sister of a rich English rancher, ostensibly for ransom money; but a close reading of the earlier manuscripts revealed another purpose. Grey wrote: "It never occurred to me that the motive [in Robber's Roost] was really rape. Most of all the present day novels are worse than rape. But I'm glad to get a chance to correct the blunder . . . . I'll gladly correct and do what's important" [to remove the suggestion of rape.[14]] Even the hint of employing themes used extensively by current literature displeased Grey.

IV Gold Fever

The discovery of gold in the Saw-Tooth Mountains of Idaho inspired two mountain novels:[15] *The Border Legion* (1916) and *Thunder Mountain* (1935). *The Border Legion* was developed from an idea given to Grey by a friend, Robert Hobart Davis. Grey, who believed the story would make a play and a strong photo-drama, asserted that "I am absolutely sure that it will be one of my stories that are read at one sitting."[16] *The Border Legion* concerned the gold rush of the 1860's at Alder Creek in Idaho. Joan Randle, originally from Missouri, quarreled with her sweetheart, Jim Cleve, causing Cleve to join outlaws headed by the notorious Jack Kells. In anguish over her deed, Joan set out to find Cleve and make amends; but, on her way, she was kidnapped by Kells. In Kells's camp, Joan, who wore a mask and masculine attire to keep her sex from being known, was nicknamed "Dandy Dale."

Joan played an ironic role in the novel. Her deeds almost turned a good man bad (Cleve) and a bad man good (Kells). When Cleve discovered who "Dandy Dale" was, his first thought was to kill her and then himself. But, when Joan convinced him that she had not been despoiled, the two made up and even slipped a parson into camp one night to marry them. Cleve and Joan, as man and wife, tried to escape from Kells and his men in the midst of a gold rush. Grey graphically described men gone mad over gold: "It was a time in which the worst of men's nature stalked forth, hydra-headed and dead, roaring for gold, spitting fire, and shedding blood. It was a time when gold and fire and blood were one . . . It was a time, for all it enriched the world with yellow treasure, when might was right, when men were hopeless, when death stalked rampant. The sun rose gold and it set red. It was the hour of Gold!" (242). Lust for gold in many men was stronger than that for a woman, so Kells's greed caused his destruction. At the novel's end, Kells and his gang shot it out with one another; and only Jim Cleve and his wife, Joan, escaped to live happily in their love for each other.

The theme of what lust for gold did to men was continued by Grey in his novel, *Thunder Mountain* (1935). At the novel's beginning, Thunder Mountain in Idaho was in a pure state of nature. First, the beavers abounded, then the Indian. While at Thunder Mountain, the Indian found gold, presaging the white man and evil days: "No voice, no warning, no spirit, no God could drive him [the white man] away." At the end of the novel, Thunder Mountain was crumbling away: "As if in mockery of the littleness of man, Nature pealed out the doom which the wise old beaver and the savage chief had foreseen—For ages its foundations had groaned warnings. And now the hour of descent had come" (282). Nature, in the fierce setting of a mountain, showed that ultimately it would prevail over the wishes of man.

The chief character was Lee (Kalispel) Emerson, one of the first white men to see gold as well as a quartz lode on Thunder Mountain. He wanted to sell the quartz lode, so he left to find a buyer. Upon his return, news of the gold supply had spread so that Thunder Mountain had grown in population, "as if by magic"; and Lee's own claim had been pre-empted. During the course of the book, Lee not only discovered a gold thief who plagued the area, but also married a dance-hall girl. The book ended with Parson Weeks at the marriage ceremony paying a ringing tribute to Western womanhood: "It is a hard country, this glorious West of ours. It takes big women to stand it . . . . They are making the West. Who shall remember in threescore years, when the broad land will be prosperous with cities and ranches, that the grandmothers of that generation, ever were, let us say, dance-hall girls? And if it were remembered, who could bring calumny against the strong-souled mothers of the West?" (298-99).

IV The Western Woman

Grey told the story of a strong-souled mother of the West in his mountain novel set in the Tonto, initially called *Frontier Wife*, but changed to *30,000 on the Hoof* (1940). This novel was one of only two mountain novels that dealt extensively with modern times, World War I and its aftermath. Actually, the novel was a saga, for it told the story of a man and his trials from the last days of Indian warfare under General George Crook to the landing of troops in France under General John Pershing. Logan Huett had stayed in Arizona after his discharge from the army in the 1880's; and he had telegraphed his proposal that Lucinda Baker in Missouri join him and become his wife. They settled in Sycamore Canyon in Arizona's Tonto Country, where Logan's great dream was to raise a herd of thirty-thousand head of cattle. He fought droughts, blizzards, grasshoppers, rustlers, and swindlers to achieve his goal. Through his ordeals, his one mainstay was his beloved wife, Lucinda. She bore him three sons, George, Abraham, and Grant. She and Logan also reared a girl named Barbara who had been lost in the Tonto and who ultimately married Logan's second son, Abe.

By the time of World War I, Logan was nearing his long-sought dream of thirty-thousand herd. When he finally sold to the government and wanted cash rather than a check, the government man filled a box full of newspapers and tinfoil and gave it to Logan; and not until some time later did Logan discover that he had been cheated out of nearly a million dollars. At about the time the government agent swindled Logan, his sons were called away to war "to make the world safe for democracy." Logan was not too apprehensive about his sons' chances until he saw a newsreel at a movie: " . . . All these scenes purported to have actually been filmed at the front made Logan sick and dazed. 'So that's war?' he muttered, jostling through the noisy crowd emerging

into the street. 'And I sent my sons into that . . . . Good God! I
reckoned they'd have a chance. Man to man, with rifles, behind
trees and rocks, where the sharp eye and crack shot would prove
who was best! But *that*—God Almighty—what would you call
that?" (254-55). Lucinda thought of the war: "Men had always,
from the remote aboriginal days, loved to fight. But it was the
women who bore sons and therefore the brunt of war . . . . She
had to face her soul now, and perhaps some day the final sacrifice of a mother, and she needed God" (236). The hateful news
finally came about her sons: George and Grant had been killed
in action, and Abe was missing. Lucinda and Huett suddenly
realized that the loss of their money to the government agent
was nought compared to the loss of their sons. The trials of Job
continued to stalk the Huett family as Barabara (Abe's wife) lost
her mind. One day, however, Abe showed up without any warning, and things began to reverse for Logan.

The United States government came very close to being the
villain in this book. Its agent cheated Logan out of his cattle
money; and, when Logan went to Washington to protest, he was
further mistreated. As if this were not bad enough, he had to sacrifice his sons to a war whose necessity for American involvement was seriously doubted by many people. The book also contained themes traditional to the mountains of the West: the
growth of manhood, perserverance, and trustworthiness. The
novel developed forcefully the theme of womanhood. Logan may
have been the strong, pioneer type, but he never would have
succeeded without Lucinda's love and moral support. Grey wanted very much to put this point into the story when he rewrote it
to enlarge the woman's perspective.[17] Dolly was quite complimentary of *30,000 on the Hoof*, calling it a "very interesting and
well written story," though it moved a bit slowly for serialization;[18] and Grey was delighted with his efforts. He wrote to Harper's requesting an early publication of *30,000 on the Hoof*, "for
which I selected a better title, *The Frontier Wife*. This is perhaps my most powerful novel and it has a tremendous climax built
around the world war and which showed what that catastrophe
did to many of our frontier people."[19]

The themes treated, the poignancy, and the style of writing
made *30,000 on the Hoof* one of Grey's best literary efforts. He
had hunted in the Tonto Country, which was the novel's setting,
and had come upon the old trail used by General Crook and also
upon the abandoned ranch of a man named Jones who had once
dreamed about a herd of thirty-thousand cattle and who raised

three sons and an adopted daughter, only to have the joys of life dashed by a horrible war.[20] Thus, the novel was about real people, real events, and real emotions.

V Grey's Popularity

Grey commented further on governmental indifference to the suffering of citizens (especially veterans) caused by World War I in his other mountain novel treating of modern times, *The Shepherd of Guadaloupe* (1930), in which Clifton Forrest, just home from the war, was shattered in body and spirit. Doctors gave him only one month to live; but it was not long before he, like other Grey characters, began improving in the New Mexico setting: "He felt, he heard, he saw, he smelled the physical objects of Nature about him" (91). Clifton found upon his return from war that his house and land had been taken by his father's old enemy, Jed Lundeen. When Lundeen's daughter, Virginia, told her father that his treatment of the Forrests was immoral, his answer was an index to the times: "Not in this day and age." Ultimately, however, right and true love won: Clifton got back his property and won Virginia's hand, putting an end to the "Forrest-Lundeen" feud that had raged for years.

Publication of *The Shepherd of Guadaloupe* in 1930 marked the twentieth anniversary of Grey's affiliation with Harper's Publishing Company. When the book's dust jacket offered a free photograph of Grey to any interested reader, hundreds of glowing tributes came from people all over the globe about Grey's power as a writer. One reader closed her letter with what was actually a compliment: "Hoping your next story is better than all the rest."[21] Another reader said: "*The Shepherd of Guadaloupe* shows that this isn't an entirely Synthetic Age [1930]— that it doesn't, in literature, take a lover and a boudoir to complete a picture of married life and that true courage isn't born of the potency of your neighbor's gin."[22] Sophisticated reviewers may have scorned Zane Grey, but the world was clearly not listening to them.

Grey produced in his mountain novels a range of themes from survival of the fittest to social commentary about the government and modern times. He was at the height of his power when many of these books were written, and this influence was apparent as he wrote in his diary in 1920 (the year *Man of the Forest* was published), "I seem to find myself a name to reckon with in the world of publishers. I have two offers, three perhaps, that are larger than any ever offered to an American writer . . . . I believe my long sought-for goal is in sight. And I shall work as never before."[23] He continued writing novels at a feverish pace throughout the 1920's. At his home in Altadena, California, he used an old morris chair with a lapboard over it to compose his stories, writing his manuscripts in pencil on legal pad paper. He also traveled extensively, but he always wrote, though sometimes sporadically, even while away from home. Some of his very popular books were written in places like Long Key, Florida; New Zealand; Central American jungles; and Australia. As Grey's fame grew, so did his confidence; but he still suffered frequently from spells of depression. His enormous output of novels in the 1920's was due, in part, to a turning point that had occurred in his career in 1918—one caused by the publication of a historical novel.

CHAPTER *4*

The Historical Novels

In a very real sense, most of Zane Grey's works were historical novels because he gave, on the whole, accurate reconstructions of the periods he wrote about. He usually took copious notes on visits to the places he described, and he profited from an association with "old timers" who actually had seen what Grey put into his novels. These firsthand accounts were often passed to Grey in distorted form; but combined with his own experiences, observations, and reading, they helped him to produce a fairly authentic picture of the Old West. For example, Grey often heard from his friend and guide, Al Doyle, stories about the building of the Union Pacific Railroad, which became the foundation for Grey's novel, *The U.P. Trail.*[1] The stories of "Buffalo" Jones, Jim Emett, John Wetherill, and many other Westerners were stored in Grey's memory, sometimes for years, and then used in his novels, short stories, and articles.[2] Grey's history depicted the epic sweep of events. Even the novels that dealt with wretched feuds implied that the reader's life was somehow better because of all the bloodshed. Grey wanted his readers to appreciate their ancestors; thus, many of his historical novels became studies in patriotism.

Grey's historical novels were based upon specific historical incidents. Building the Union Pacific Railroad, Boulder Dam, and Western Union, are well attested feats in the history of this country. The frequent lack of humanity toward Indians, the widespread activity of the International Workers of the World both during and after World War I, the occurrence of range wars, the passing of the buffalo, and the fight against predatory economic interests are also well documented. Through his research, Grey discussed these points in most of his other novels, but in the historical novels, they became the central focal point—the moving force of the novels themselves.

I   The History of a Railroad

In *The U.P. Trail* (1918), Grey's first historical novel dealing with the West, he depicted the building of the Union Pacific Railroad as a "work of giants," and he desired that his novel embrace "all that could be possible during that wild time and colossal enterprise."[3] In the course of the railroad's construction, it came to mean different things to different people: to Warren Neale, engineer, it was a dream; to several railroad commissioners like Allison Lee, it was a source of profit; to Slingerland the trapper, it was the end of America's great wilderness;[4] and to the Indian, it was the death-knell of his way of life.

The main character, Warren Neale, an Easterner, was young and idealistic; he believed he was participating in an event of world-wide significance, and he could not understand why some men thought differently: "Why could not all men be right-minded about a noble cause and work unselfishly for the development of the West and the future generations?" (106). Neale spent much time thwarting the purposes of profiteers and lamenting the underhanded tactics of the construction companies—primarily the Credit Mobilier—which had contracted to build the railroad. On the surface, building the Union Pacific Railroad may have been one of the most adventurous and romantic episodes in American history, but underneath all the show was a grasping bureaucracy mired in the depths of corruption. One of the greatest despoilers was Commissioner Lee; ironically, Neale loved his daughter, Allie.

Neale and his sidekick, Larry Red King (who turned out to be the brother of the notorious Texas gunman, Kingfisher) had found Allie after an Indian attack in which she had been the only survivor. Just before Allie's mother had died in the Indian raid she told Allie the truth about her father—that she was the daughter of Commissioner Lee. Neale and Larry Red King nursed Allie back to health, both fell in love with her, but Allie preferred Neale. Later, Allie was kidnapped by gambler Durade, her mother's second husband, and forcibly kept at his gambling saloon at the head of the railroad, a wild place named Benton, where life was cheap indeed. Before Allie was rescued from the gambling saloon, several men were killed, including Larry Red King. When Allie was safe and reunited with her father, all should have been well for Allie and Neale, but nothing was further from the truth. Her father doubted Neale's morals since Neale had publicly befriended Beauty Stanton, operator of a local saloon, and had fought Allison over operations of the

Union Pacific Railroad. Allie was sent to Omaha where she stayed for months yearning for her lover. Finally, she could bear it no longer, so she left her father for Warren Neale.

Allie found Neale at Promontory Point, Utah, where the last spikes of the transcontinental railroad were about to be driven. Arizona donated a spike of gold, silver and iron for the occasion; Nevada, one of silver; and California; one of pure gold. Thousands of people, including the famed Irish builders, gathered around to witness the historic event. The driving of the last spike was to be heard all over the country by telegraphic facilities, after which the vast audience would shout "DONE!" to a waiting world. Neale's heart was full as he watched these proceedings; to him, the scene was "great, beautiful, final." He had a tremendous sense of fulfillment, and the only thing missing was his beloved Allie. But, in the middle of the ceremonies, Neale felt a small hand in his; he looked around and there was Allie! His triumph was complete.

II   A Turning Point in Grey's Career

The U.P. Trail represented a personal triumph for Grey, because it marked an important turning point in his career. Before 1918, Grey had regarded his Western novels and short stories as "stepping stones to a higher plane of literature." His "apprenticeship" in the Western field was preparation for the Great American Novel, in which the psychological aspects of youth would be fully explored. The success of *The U.P. Trail*, however, and the personal exuberance that its thrust gave to Grey caused his decision to stay solely in Westerns and adventure stories: "My power and my study and passion shall be directed to that which already I have written best—the beauty and color and mystery of great spaces, of the open, of Nature in her wild moods. This decision has been a relief."[5]

Not only did Grey put these thoughts about *The U.P. Trail* into his diary, he also wrote essentially the same things to Hitchcock at Harper's: "Much good has come to me, in the way of significant appreciation, since *The U.P. Trail* was published. It is like wine."[6] Grey's decision was quickly applauded by Hitchcock and the other editors at Harper's, who had no desire to lose their most popular writer. In still another letter, Grey said in relation to *The U.P. Trail*: "All these years my idea has been to win a public, and then write the powerful psychological novels of love, passion, and tragedy, that I am capable of writing . . . .

For long I have been divided between this course, and of throwing all my study and work, passion and power, into what I really do best—an interpretation of Nature."[7] Having made this important decision about his writing, Grey wavered only once, in 1922, when he allowed the non-Western novel, *The Day of the Beast*, to be published. Significantly, that book was one of the least successful he ever wrote.

Grey apparently found 1918 the year to express the courage of his convictions. Not only did he come to a basic decision regarding the type of literature he would write, he also publicized his violent anti-Germanism. World War I upset the world's equilibrium, and Grey blamed the Germans. In April, 1917, he recorded in his diary: "We are on the eve of war with Germany and the soldiers have been sent all over the U.S. to guard bridges, water-powers, and public buildings. Meanwhile, there is hell in Washington, excitement all over the country . . . . I am perhaps as far as any man from wanting war. Yet I come from a family of fighters . . . . I am no pacifist—no peace at any price man. . . . I hate war more than I hate anything else. The agony to women and children I cannot forgive."[8] By the close of the following year, Grey's feelings against the Germans had grown to vitriolic proportions: "Right has prevailed over the Brute, but after effects are deadly. Famine stalks abroad . . . . Germans should not pay in gold—but in blood."[9] With these viewpoints toward the Germans, it was easily predictable that Grey would write a novel dealing with the World War, *The Desert of Wheat*.

III Grey Versus the "Wobblies"

Grey, accompanied by Dolly, visited the wheat-growing areas of Washington State in preparation for writing *The Desert of Wheat* (1919). While there, he read scientific articles about wheat diseases; and he also familiarized himself with the operations of the International Workmen of the World (I.W.W.), clipping long newspaper passages about the "Wobblies" to his manuscript.[10] His trip and his studies were significant enough for several newspapers to write stories about them; thus, the American reading public was prepared for an anti-German novel from Grey.

The novel's setting was the "Bend" country in Washington in 1917, just after the United States had entered the war against Germany. There were two dramatic conflicts in the book: first was Kurt Dorn's argument with his German-born father, who believed that the United States was being led astray by England; and this father-son confrontation caused Kurt to have guilt feelings about his German background. The second conflict occurred between the area's wheat farmers and the I.W.W., who wanted to undermine the growth of agricultural products for use by the United States military forces.

Grey treated the "Wobblies" as a corrupt labor union at best, as spies for the Germans at worst. The organization intimidated farm workers, causing many to walk off their jobs; and it threw phosphorus cakes into wheat fields which ignited through the hot rays of the sun. While fighting such a fire, Kurt's father died of a heart attack. Just before he expired, he admitted his errors in blindly supporting the German cause. The situation improved considerably after a group of concerned citizens decided to deal with the I.W.W. in the "good old Western way": they hanged the "Wobbly" leader and left his body tied to a railroad trestle where everybody—friend and foe—could see it. The sight tempered activist plans by the I.W.W.

The war caused Kurt Dorn to suffer inner conflicts. The area's residents tried to convince him that he could best serve his country by staying at home and raising wheat; but he could not do that, no matter its importance. The war had become a very personal thing to him; he had, it seemed, a debt that he must pay for his German origins. When he joined the army, his reasons were mostly personal. Even the woman he loved, Lenore Anderson, could not dissuade him from this course of action. In combat, Kurt did not experience the thrill from inflicting his first casualty that he had imagined he would: "His life on earth, his spirit in the beyond, could never be now what they might have been. And he sobbed through grinding teeth as he felt the disintegrating, agonizing, irremediable forces at work on body, mind, and soul" (323). His fatalism caused him to become a hero in an advance against the Germans, but he was wounded so seriously that a specialist gave him only a short time to live. Kurt took his discharge and went home to Washington; there trying to fathom life in general, and his own in particular, Kurt thought: "What were wounds, blood, mangled flesh, agony, and death to men—to those who went out for liberation of something unproven in themselves? Life was only a breath. The secret must lie in the beyond, for men could not act that way for nothing" (348).

When Lenore Anderson nursed Kurt back to health, she grew pensive about the role of womanhood in war. In the original manuscript of *The Desert of Wheat* Grey stated (but later deleted) the problem that war presented to woman; "They [women] were cursed with lesser bodies [than men] and blessed with higher souls. War was night, hell and devastation to women . . . . If materialistic war meant the survival of the fittest in the evolution of the race, sacrifices of mothers to that inscrutable design running through the ages was made to be only a monstrous lie, an animal function abhorrent and base . . ."[11] In the published work, Grey gave women's solution to the problem of war: they should band together and refuse to have children. This denial to the male ego would cause a miraculous change in the occurrence of wars: thus "would come an end to violence, to greed, to hate, to war, to the black and hideous imperfection of mankind" (353). Lenore fulfilled the requirements of a Grey heroine by nursing Kurt back to health, by marrying him, and then by becoming his major source of strength.

The Desert of Wheat was lauded by reviewer Theodore Brooke in *Harper's Magazine*. He liked Grey's treatment of the hero, Kurt Dorn, who had to fight not only with "musket and muscles" but also with mind and soul. The heroine came off better, in Brooke's opinion, than in Grey's previous novels.[12] The tribute to *The Desert of Wheat* that Grey liked best, however, was the one his native Zanesville paid it when he went home in 1921: "I was sought, praised, flattered, entertained as never before in my life. I belonged to Zanesville. I was a Zane, and these people, my old friends, and many new ones, are proud of me. The reception filled me with awe, wonder, sadness & gratitude."[13] As a special honor to Grey, the movie based on the novel was played in the town's cinema. Though Dolly had stated previously that the movie suffered from a marked departure from the book[14] its showing while Grey was in Zanesville provided some poignant moments for him.

The most nostalgic moment for Grey, however, in that 1921 homecoming occurred as he walked down a street and saw this poem in a store window:

"Come along with me Mr. Gray [*sic*]
We'll go fishing at Dillon's today,
Forget 'Betty Zane' and all the rest
For a day of the sport you used to love best.
For all the honors they've paid you, I ween
You'd gladly exchange for one glimpse of that scene.
The 'Plains' and 'The Rockies' bow low to your pen
But the Muskingum and Licking are calling again

There's 'Cannon Hell' Putnam and old Cedar Rock
And the Swimmin' hole! down by the old steam-boat lock.
The 'diamond' up at the old White House ground,
Say, boy, shall I stop or how does it sound?"

The author, C. M. Shrider, a young storeclerk, had pieced together Grey's old haunts by talking to Grey's contemporaries.[15]
Grey tenderly remembered the incident for the rest of his life.

IV Activity on the Rogue

Grey's pre-occupation with World War I continued in *Rogue
River Feud*, a novel that was serialized in 1929 by *Country Gentleman* under the title *Rustlers of Silver River*. The story's main
character was Kevin Bell, a part of whose jaw had been shot away
in combat. He faced a different kind of struggle when he became
a civilian and fought a big canning company in Oregon for using
illegally sized nets to catch salmon at the mouth of the Rogue
River. Bell also hated the timber barons who indiscriminately
destroyed the redwood trees of California and the white cedars
of Oregon. Although Bell was denied any help from the government for his war-sustained injuries, the government regularly
voted advantages in the form of tax breaks, and even subsidies,
to the predatory business interests in this country. Such a condition embittered people like Kevin Bell and his partner, Garry
Lord.

As to be expected, the love of a good woman saved Kevin Bell;
for Beryl Aard showed him the uselessness of brooding over past
failures. Life was meant to be lived happily. Ultimately, through
perseverance, Kevin got the illegally operating canneries investi-
gated and activities of corrupt law officials looked into. He concluded at the book's end that the "feud" had been mostly with
himself. He was still embittered from the war and from his experiences thereafter, so much so that he said he would fight again
only if the country were under direct physical invasion, but
would continue to combat despoilers. He attained personal happiness through Beryl's love, showing that one must somehow
find a balance between life as it is, and life as it is wished.

As in *30,000 on the Hoof*, the federal government was largely
the villain of *Rogue River Feud*. Grey was not anti-government,
but he definitely questioned many of its procedures. Why allow
grasping profiteers to destroy the beauty and the resources of
the country—not only allow, but help—while thousands of war
veterans went without? This action was a mark of great ingrati-

tude, one that badly needed correcting. He wrote on this subject to Dolly: "The times are bad. The war left greed, selfishness, lawlessness, and crookedness paramount in the hearts of almost all men. I fear my patriotism has been dealt a blow from which it will never recover."[16] Grey's continued stance of social commentator dictated against his being merely a "writer of Western novels."

V A Famous Feud

Grey achieved additional recognition as a historical novelist by writing about a different kind of feud from the one involving government and big business. *To The Last Man* (1922), a copiously researched novel, delved deeply into the Graham-Tewksbury feud which started in Texas and ended in the Tonto Country of Arizona.[17] In Tonto history it was known as the Pleasant Valley War and as something of a "feud within a feud," for it involved personal hatred between two families in the context of a cattleman-sheepman war. Grey changed the name to the "Jorth-Isbel feud." During the Civil War, Gaston Isbel served in the Confederate army; in his absence, Lee Jorth courted and married Isbel's sweetheart. Thus, the basis was laid for a feud that ultimately affected several generations.

The book's only heroic characters were women. Ellen Jorth wanted to be true to her father's side in the feud, but she needed love as well. (Her mother had died years ago.) When she met Jean Isbel, she hated him—on the surface. But his presence caused her unconsciously to feel the need and desire of loving and of being loved: "It was new, sensorial life, elemental, primitive, a liberation of a million inherited instincts, quivering and physical, over which Ellen had no . . . control . . . ." Not understanding this sudden rush of sensations, Ellen wanted to be hidden, "covered by green thicket, lost in the wildness of Nature, unconsciously seeking a Mother" (230). Theodore Brooke, reviewing *To the Last Man* for *Harper's Magazine*, tended to make Ellen's path to love with Jean Isbel the most important thing in the novel: "Grey reveals new powers which even his stanchest admirers could never dream he possessed. There is a delicacy of touch in his handling of Ellen which enables him to look deep into the heart of the Motherless girl men called a 'hussy.' "[18] Ellen was as close to Nature as any character Grey ever created, and symbolized the primitivism of that wild country. Yet, love, man's paramount emotion, was the final victor.

Ellen and Jean, members of a younger generation of Jorths and Isbels, were caught—like Shakespeare's Romeo and Juliet—in a cruel dilemma. Logic told them that the feud was wrong but a sense of loyalty tied them to their families. They were forced to walk a tightrope of indecision until most of the warring factions were destroyed, and they could freely express their love for each other. Unlike the couple in the most famous feud story of all time, Ellen and Jean were not "star-crossed": the combination of a Zane Grey Romance and a country that could be called "the land of the happy ending" dictated against ultimate tragedy for the young lovers.

Grey used a horrifying incident to extol the virtues and bravery of womanhood. When the Jorths one day besieged the Isbels, two of the Isbel faction were killed before they could take cover. While their bodies lay in a field, the Jorths turned loose a herd of hogs who headed straight for the corpses. When the women in the beleaguered Isbel camp exhorted the men to recover the bodies and all refused, two women braved Jorth fire to put their men into shallow, temporary graves to keep them from being eaten by the swine. The deed was so brave that it caused a cease-fire by the feuders, who looked on in awe. Thus, base man was sharply contrasted with noble woman.

After the Jorth-Isbel feud had passed into history when the last of the major participants were killed, Ellen and Jean found a common enemy—an outlaw named Colton who rode for the notorious Hash Knife Outfit and who used the feud as a front for his evil deeds. He was finally killed by Jean Isbel, thus erasing the last barrier to Ellen and Jean's marriage. *To The Last Man* was largely a psychological study of a feud mentality, for the struggle had continued long after most people had forgotten the reason for it. Vanity was the disease that propelled it; love, the quality that stopped it. It may be that Grey's former wish to write a great psychological novel never quite left him despite his disavowals of it after *The U.P. Trail* was published. Perhaps *To The Last Man* was, in part, a tribute to that subconscious desire. If so, the psychological-historical combination within a Western setting produced a quite significant piece of work.

VI *The Passing of the Buffalo*

Feuds and range wars, frequent occurrences in the Old West, marked the violence of the time and place; and they ended the career of more than one illustrious person. Billy the Kid, for example, was slain as a result of New Mexico's Lincoln County War, alluded to, but never fully treated, in several of Grey's novels. Grey wanted to encompass the entire range of human experience in the West—to capture on paper man's splendor in one instance and his greed in another. Expressive of greed was a historical novel by Grey, *The Thundering Herd* (1925), which is not unlike *To the Last Man* for its extreme violence and for the delineation of man's less noble instincts. *The Thundering Herd* was the story of the buffalo, and the tragedy of its passing. Grey, who had been interested in the historical aspects of the great buffalo slaughter ever since his association with "Buffalo" Jones, told in his novel of the carnage, and showed, in no uncertain terms, how man was debased by it.

Many professional hunters were convinced that they were serving civilization when they went by the thousands into the Staked Plains of Texas and New Mexico. They were opening the Southwest for farmers and cattlemen—a feat that not even the United States army could accomplish. The Indian threat decreased in proportion to the number of buffalo killed; and more than 200,000 buffalo hides from the Southwest herd were shipped East in 1876; and later the bones were picked up and sold for fertilizer. Only the Indians regarded the buffalo as a major food supply—one reason the government made no effort to stop the wanton destruction of the bison herds. With the source of food exhuasted, the Indians became dependent on, and subservient to, the federal government and were forced to accept reservation life.

In the novel, a woman, Millie Fayre, saw the abject horror of the buffalo slaughter; and she entreated her sweetheart, Tom Doan, to give up the business—indeed, she made relinquishing it a condition of her marriage to him. Tom swore to comply with Millie's wishes as soon as he had earned enough money to buy a ranch. One day, however, Tom had to kill a motherless young buffalo: "This incident boded ill for Tom. It fixed his mind on this thing he was doing and left him no peace. Thousands and thousands of beautiful little buffalo calves were rendered motherless by the hide-hunters. That was to Tom the unforgivable brutality" (373). Tom ultimately concluded that buffalo hunters were degraded by the wholesale slaughter, for nature had not meant for such fearful events to occur. Tom, however, was in a distinct minority in forming this conclusion; but Millie Fayre hastened his decision to give up buffalo hunting.

Grey was personally dissatisfied with *The Thundering Herd*

when he finished writing it: "I do not feel that I have done
well in writing of this romance of the buffalo. Always I have
that feeling at the end of work. I seemed to have failed of the
great epic strife I set out to picture."[19] He wanted the book to
be a social force, as he indicated when he wrote an account of
it to the readers of *Boy's Magazine*: "I hope you boys, and all
my readers, will be interested in the story, not only because I
have tried to draw a true picture of the extermination of one of
the most wonderful of our own American animals, but also that
it may give you the impulse toward conservation of what wild life
still exists in our great country."[20]

One reason, possibly, that Grey was not too pleased with *The
Thundering Herd* was that the editors wanted him to change the
novel's ending to give greater depth to the characters.[21] Characterization did not come too easily to Grey in any circumstance,
and his attempted improvement of it in *The Thundering Herd*
was a failure. He continually told the editors that the book was
a saga of the buffalo; therefore, characterization was deliberately minimized. A second reason for trouble with *The Thundering
Herd* was that fiction in 1925 was in a weakened condition; for
general entertainment trends veered away from the literary
world as radios, automobiles, and movies became the most popular diversions of the day. Publishing fiction became so compet-
itive that an editor expressed the opinion that "even Zane Grey
cannot afford to have a 'flivver.' "[22] At approximately the time
that this dialogue took place about *The Thundering Herd*, another
of Grey's books touched off a controversy; and this was the novel
that Grey told a friend he would like to be remembered by, *The
Vanishing American*.

VII *Grey's Famous Indian Novel*

Zane Grey as a social agitator never came off better than in
The Vanishing American (1925). Long sympathetic to the Indian,
Grey drew a poignant and stark portrait of the Red Man; but, in
doing so, he gave offense to several religious groups in the United
States and also to the Bureau of Indian Affairs.

The setting was the Nopah Reservation[23] during the era of
World War I. The chief character was Nophaie who, when just
a babe, was kidnapped by white men and then turned loose to
wander in the wilderness. Some wealthy Easterners found him,
reared him, and gave him a white man's education. In college
he was "Lo Blandy," a great scholar and athlete; and his sweet-

heart was Marian Warner, whom he called "Benow di Cleash." After graduation, Marian visited the Reservation, to which Nophaie had returned, and there she witnessed tragic events.

The Indian Reservation was a gallery of horrors. A man named Blucher, a German, was head of it. When America entered the war in 1917, Blucher, showing clearly his sympathy with the German cause, discouraged Indians from volunteering. The head of the missionary force on the Reservation was Morgan, a cruel and wicked man, who always hid his baseness behind the "Old Book" and committed crime after crime in its name. Behind these two people was a coterie of disreputable associates. Grey said of the Indian agents: "They were holding down an irksome job; they were out there because they had failed in the East or for poor health or because they had political influence enough to gain a job they were not equal to . . . . Some there were who had honestly tried hard to adopt themselves to this work, only to find it beyond them" (150). Of the missionaries, Grey wrote: "The sincere missionary, the man who left home and comfort and friends to go into a lonely hard country, burning with zeal to convey the blessings of Jesus Christ to those he considered heathen, had little conception of the true nature of his task, of the absurdity of converting Indians in a short time . . . . How little did the world outside a reservation know of this tremendous and staggering question! The good missionary's life was a martyrdom" (151).

Caught between the inept forces of the Indian Bureau on one hand and the misguided efforts of missionary boards on the other, the life of the Reservation Indian was sad indeed. Few people listened to Nophaie's suggestions that people like Morgan be removed, that the Indian be given land to work, that the Indian send his children to school where he wished, and that Indians move freely among whites. In the context of these forlorn conditions events occurred of grotesque proportions. The Indians resisted Morgan's rule that children attend church in his chapel, and were harshly reprimanded for their opinions. In World War I, the Indian was subjected to further abuse by the "bunko game" of having to adopt some general into a tribe; such a deed, said Grey, was usually a cheap political trick to keep some person in power. As if Indian agents and missionaries were not enough, the post-war influenza epidemics exacted fearful tolls upon the tribes, for over three thousand Nopahs, to say nothing of the other tribes, died from influenza. Nophaie caught the dread disease, but recovered.

Nophaie represented a threat to white authority on the Reservation. He had been educated in a white man's college, but he had ultimately rejected the white man's life. Usually a white-educated Indian did not pose such a problem, because once educated, an Indian could never return to the old tribal beliefs and superstitions on the one hand, but could never win acceptance from the white community. The frustration resulting from such a condition usually turned the Indian into a nonentity; but this development, however, did not apply to Nophaie. If anything, the white-man's education enabled him to draw a sharp contrast between the primitive, natural, pure life of his youth and the so-called progress of twentieth-century America. He rebelled against the white ideal of progress, and he suffered as a result. Despite his rebellion, he loved a white woman. Marian Warner returned his love, but the accumulated tragedies affecting their lives boded ill for its fulfillment.

The book ended with Nophaie, having recovered from influenza, making a pilgrimage in gratitude to Naza, a sacred bridge that had been a symbol of the Indians' pantheistic religion for generations. The trek to and from it was excruciating; but Nophaie got there, and he found God, his God, not the white man's. When he returned to the Reservation where Marian was waiting for him, he was so weakened by his exhausting journey, that he again fell ill. This time he did not recover; and he was, therefore, a symbol of the vanishing American. This novel was the only one that Grey ever wrote with a Western setting that did not end on a happy note. From the point of style, balance, and emotions it evoked, it was, perhaps, his best book.

It took Grey from May 5 to June 18, 1922, to write *The Vanishing American*. On the last stretch of its writing, he labored for fourteen consecutive hours; but he did not suffer the usual negative reactions when he had completed it—"I went the whole distance with this novel without one day of depression, let alone bad spell."[24] Perhaps his stability was due to his decision to write and fish on alternate days. When the book first appeared in 1922 as a serial in *Ladies' Home Journal*, it came under attack from several religious sources. When plans were announced for Harper's to publish the book and for a movie based on it to be released simultaneously, some denominations feared a general muckraking attack on missionaries. When the editor of *Ladies' Home Journal* wrote to Harper's of the controversy caused by serializing *The Vanishing American*, he expressed the opinion that adverse comments were not sufficient to affect publication of the book.[25] Even so, Grey still went through a trying time relative to the planned appearances of the book and movie.

The Harper editors suggested a number of changes in *The Vanishing American*. One related to the internal construction of the novel: Grey should change the time of Nophaie's death to give the book a climax equal to its opening,[26] and he complied with this request. As time passed, however, it became obvious, at least to Grey, that Harper's was reluctant to publish the book for fear of offending church people. This hesitation angered Grey, and he stated that he would withdraw his manuscript but for the planned simultaneous appearances of the book and the movie.[27] He was inclined to be a "little sore," he said, because this was the first time he had "ever bucked up against the Church or religious element. I begin to understand a little of the narrow controversy between modernists and fundamentalists."[28] Grey stated his position in a long, often impassioned, letter to the publishing company.

He wrote just after his third revision of the manuscript: "I have studied the Navajo Indians for twelve years. I know their wrongs. The missionaries sent out there are almost everyone mean, vicious, weak, immoral, useless men . . ." and then, in a blaze of anti-climax, he added, ". . . and some of them are crooks. They cheat and rob the Indian and more heinously they seduce every Indian girl they can get hold of. It is common knowledge on the reservation. And mind you this is only the Navajo Reservation. My purpose was to expose this terrible condition—to help the great public to understand the Indian's wrongs."[29] Grey expressed doubts in this letter that religious people read his books to any extent; even if they did, "I would want them to read what I wrote as the truth about missionaries and their wrongs to the Indian. If it offended them—no matter. If it aroused a controversy—well and good. But in any event it was my record of a certain phase of American Western history. Eventually, it was going to be believed. The *truth* always comes out."[30] Grey closed his letter by asserting that recent official disclosures about the Indian board and the current debate in religious circles on modernism and fundamentalism made 1924 the psychological time to publish *The Vanishing American*.

Grey ultimately got most of what he wanted in his book; but his troubles with it were not yet over. The movie producers gave him some bad moments. Grey complained during the filming that the book and the movie were too far apart from each other. He insisted that the action and spirit of his books be put on the screen and that the moviemakers "interpolate something of the poetry and legend of the Indian."[31] These and similar requests reduced to negligibility some critics' charges that Grey wrote only for the movies.

VIII   The West: Repository of Greatness

The last of Grey's works published during his lifetime was also a historical novel, *Western Union* (1939), which concerned the telegraph, another development that changed life, especially the Indian's. When Grey had attempted to dictate stories as early as 1918, he gave up the practice as impracticable; but much of *Western Union* was dictated because a stroke two years before had altered his writing habits. The infirmity did not keep Grey from thoroughly researching his subject, and the novel contained a solid account of the trials encountered while installing transcontinental telegraphic facilities. Grey wrote his book in the first person, and dedicated it to a "single thread of wire" running across the country. Aside from characterization, which was often weak in Grey novels, *Western Union* was strong in organization, balance of events, and historical authenticity.

The story's narrator was Wayne Cameron, an idealistic young Easterner who, like Warren Neale of the Union Pacific Railroad of a later period, believed he was privileged to participate in spectacular events. In constructing the line in 1861, the crews encountered several problems; and one of these was Indian raids by the Cheyenne, Arapaho, and Utes. A stage driver named Hawkins gave the Indian's point of view: the idea of progress was good, he said, "but it doesn't do 'way with the fact thet this was the red man's country, thet he was depraved by liquor, thet he has been robbed, an' will go on bein' robbed until what's left of him will be driven back into the waste places of the West. Jest how it is in the sight of God, I cain't reckon. But in mine it shore ain't a purty picture" (7-8). Hawkins may have been the character in the book making the statement, but Zane Grey was speaking.

Another difficulty which the telegraph crews faced was timber rustlers—people who constantly claimed that Western Union had illegally cut timber from their homesteads; and Cameron spent much time invalidating their charges. Buffalo stampedes continually threatened the men and their outfits. When, to protect newly installed poles from animals, the Chief Engineer, Edward Creighton, put spikes around them, he did not anticipate buffaloes coming along and scratching their backs on the spikes to get rid of the mud and vermin on them. More than twenty-five miles of poles were destroyed before the error was discovered. In addition to Indians, rustlers and buffaloes, nature challenged the telegraph stringers, mostly in the form of floods and electrical storms. But the event was too big, too promising, for any force, individually or collectively, to destroy it: "Its meaning was tremendous. Thousands of men and women from the South and East had become imbued with the hope of finding a better life in the West, and fired with this pioneer spirit they had pulled up their roots and started across the Plains. It was the beginning of a great empire in the West" (155).

Western Union had the usual number of Grey type characters in it who indulged in the now familiar melodrama of his novels. As in most instances, however, the thing with Grey in *Western Union* was the setting and the event, not the characters. The sweep of events, the whole of which was greater than the sum of its parts, motivated Grey; for he wanted people to experience a surge of nationalism when reading his historical novels. *Western Union* ended on a patriotic note when the first message transmitted was from California's Chief Justice who pledged his state's loyalty to President Lincoln in the Civil War which had just started. The telegraph figured prominently in the ultimate Union victory, so Grey did not overlook its importance in holding the Union together. Indeed, the string of wire became a symbol of the great strength and fortitude of the United States.

Grey tended to make huge construction projects symbolic of America's progress in the world, and denotative of super-human efforts in which ordinary men would find no place. The Union Pacific Railroad and Western Union were excellent examples of this aspect of Grey's thoughts. Another feat that required extraordinary men—not just in terms of building, but of idealism as well—was the construction of Hoover Dam on the Nevada-Arizona border. After its completion, its name was changed to Boulder Dam, and then several years later, it re-acquired its original name. When Grey wrote his novel, it was called Boulder Dam, the name he used for the title of his novel. Hoover Dam, the greatest water barrier in the world and one of history's greatest engineering accomplishments,[32] attracted world-wide attention as armies of engineers, drillers, dynamiters, and steam-shovelers converged on the scene to harness the powers of the Colorado River. The project turned Las Vegas, Nevada, into a boom town that belittled even the frenzied days of frontiers and gold rushes.

The book's hero, Lynn Weston, was not an Easterner like War-

ren Neale of the Union Pacific or Wayne Cameron of Western
Union. Weston did come, however, from a wealthy California
family that threatened his individuality. Thus, just as Boulder
Dam personified a nation's greatness, it symbolized manhood
for Lynn personally. Since he wanted to run the entire gauntlet
of experience at the dam, he was a sand and gravel man for a
time, then a steam-shoveler, a cliff driller, a scaler, and finally,
a supervisor. The work was invigorating, intriguing, and perilous.

The greatest threat to the dam, however, did not come from
natural sources: Communists began underhanded work to ham-
per, or even prevent, the dam's construction. Grey, always a con-
servative author, distrusted anything that hinted of a marked
change in tradition; therefore, he fought against Communist in-
filtration, real or imagined. He wrote in a letter in 1934 of his belief that Communists inspired the labor strikes in San Francisco,
and he thought the authorities should "deal summarily with that
element."[33] In *Boulder Dam*, Grey summarized his thoughts
through the words of Lynn Weston: "These damn Reds! Had they
gotten a foothold here in this greatest and best paid labor project
ever conceived? What was the United States coming to?" (177).
The book was full of hectic chases in which Lynn Weston fought
both Communists and gangsters. In the end, a "reformed" gangster helped Lynn to rescue his girl, Anne Vandergrift, from Communist criminal elements.[34] Thus, the story ended on a happy
note, with Grey musing about man's genius in building the dam.

Time, however, was on nature's side, so Grey wondered how
long it would be before nature reclaimed that which man had
taken from her. Grey was awed by the magnitude of the under-
taking, and he stood in reverence at this accomplishment of man;
but he could not quite bring himself to the point of allowing man
to get away with Boulder Dam. He sprinkled his narrative with
references to the fact that the Colorado existed long before man
had, and would probably outlast him. Even a mighty structure
like Boulder Dam was only a transient thing in the grand scheme
of eternity.

From the Union Pacific Railroad to Boulder Dam, Grey revealed the West as America's best repository for greatness. The
West encouraged manliness; it followed, then, that manly things
be built and that manly events take place. The West became the
proving ground for the splendor of the nation and for the matu-
rity of the individual. Grey overdrew this picture several times,
but the total result of his work was acceptable historical and social

comment. *The Vanishing American*, for example, was comparable to Helen Hunt Jackson's *Ramona*; and it was written in the same vein as Upton Sinclair's *The Jungle*. Perhaps *The Vanishing American* did not influence governmental policy so much as *The Jungle*, but it did make thousands of fair-minded people take notice of the Indian problem for the first time. *Rogue River Feud* undoubtedly had its effects, too, upon those people whose job was to encourage fair business practices.

In respect to these questions of setting the social order straight, Grey's influence may have been greater than has been supposed. Grey believed, apparently, that history was at its best when it applied to contemporary problems, thus becoming a social force. History could never predict events, but it could offer a number of alternatives and indicate which one was likely to be best. Thus, Grey's historical novels, for all of their overwriting, did contain some significant suggestions for the betterment of human conditions.

CHAPTER 5

Horses

When Christopher Columbus made a second voyage to the New World in 1493, he brought with him a number of stallions, mares, and mules. When Hernando Cortez invaded Mexico twenty-five years later, he took with him from Cuba the descendants of those animals and introduced horseflesh to the mainland of the North American continent. Several years after this occurrence, the Spanish explorer, Francisco Coronado, wandered throughout the country now known as the American Southwest; and, during this expedition, he abandoned or lost many of his horses. These animals were the ancestors of all the multitudes of horses that ultimately roamed the Western regions; and, without horseflesh, Western development would have been much more difficult than it was, if not impossible. The horse was literally the difference sometimes between life and death for a person. It was not unusual for a horse to attain a high degree of intelligence—sometimes, apparently, even higher than that of its owner. A horse generally had great stamina, and it brought men through difficulties that alone they could not have overcome. Little wonder, then, that the Westerner's love for his horse often surpassed any affections he had for gold or for women—or that one of the most serious crimes was to steal a man's horse.

Very early in Grey's career as a recorder of Western history, he appreciated the value of a horse. In *The Last of the Plainsmen*, Grey sang the praises of horseflesh as he described the futile efforts of mere humans to capture "Silvermane," king of the wild horses. The great stallion was subdued only in the pages of *The Heritage of the Desert*, becoming, as it were, one of the book's leading characters. By 1912 Grey owned several horses, and his favorites Black Star and Night figured prominently in *Riders of the Purple Sage*. Blanco Diablo, and Blanco Sol, two more of Grey's horses, were featured in *Desert Gold*. He became an astute observer of horses, writing into his notebooks descriptions of their habits, of their fortitude, and of their nobility. Horses played an important role in the majority of Grey's novels, and the horse itself was the central character in two.

I *Wildfire*

The first of Grey's "horse" novels was *Wildfire*, serialized by *Country Gentleman* in 1916, and published as a book the following year. Grey was becoming, in 1917, a celebrated man of letters; and *Wildfire* was enthusiastically received by readers—so much so that Hitchcock informed Grey that *Wildfire* had surpassed all of Harper's expectations.[1] The novel's setting was the canyon country of Northern Arizona, just south of the Utah border; and the time was the late nineteenth century, when the cattle industry had made the horse such a valuable creature that most Western states had passed laws stipulating capital punishment for horse-thieves.

A major part of the story dealt with the "Bostil-Creech feud," started because of a dispute over horses. Bostil, a sane man on everything but horses, robbed, lied, and cheated to get a horse that he wanted. At one time he and Creech were good friends, but a horsetrade turned them into bitter enemies. Bostil could have no friends if any conversations revolved (as they usually did) around horses. Bostil even cut the lines to the ferryboat one night to keep Creech's horses from being transported across the river to participate in a race. The deed was a hollow victory for Bostil, though, because the rains came, causing the river to flood and maroon the horses. Before the waters receded, Creech's horses had starved to death, a turn of events that was most disheartening to a lover of horseflesh.

Bostil was not the only, or even the most intense, horse lover in the novel, just the most malignant. His daughter Lucy tormented Bostil by taunting him over the supposed superiority of his favorite horse, Sage King. Lucy encouraged Slone, a wild-horse trapper, to run newly captured Wildfire in a race against Sage King. During the event, the two horses fought each other so much that no clear-cut decision was established. As Lucy expected, Bostil coveted Wildfire, causing animosities to develop between himself and Slone. To complicate matters, Slone and Lucy fell in love with each other. Bostil hinted on numerous occasions that he was not beyond trading his beloved daughter for the magnificent horse.

Before Bostil was forced to make a choice, Lucy was kidnapped by Creech and his son Joel. On the trail, father and son quarreled over the treatment of their victim; and Joel shot his father. Maddened, Joel stripped Lucy naked, tied her to the back of Sage King, and set the grass afire. At this point, Slone appeared on the scene; and a terrific race ensued between Wildfire and Sage King. Wildfire won, but he had exerted himself so much that he died of exhaustion. Slone's recovery of Lucy won Bostil's gratitude, causing Bostil to reflect on his past selfishness, and leading to his promise of better citizenship on the subject of horses.

Grey used a horse in this novel to get at the peculiar characteristics of the human element, for he recognized that a lucid person could be insane, or obsessed, about one particular thing. Bostil was of two personalities: one that dealt with people and one that dealt with horses. Grey read enough of Clayton Hamilton's *Manual of Fiction* to know that characters must always act within the laws of their imagined existence; that the rules of life, not the author's will, must decide the destinies of heroes and heroines; and that characters must be typical of the class to which they belong.[2] Under these conditions in a good work of fiction, the characters became as true as real life. Bostil was a case in point because he typified the thoughts of so many Westerners about horses.

The horse, Wildfire, became a pivot point for the expression of several different feelings. The great steed inspired in Bostil an overpowering sense of competition through which he could gain power over men. Wildfire created a challenge for Slone in that it took him several months and near-fatal exertion to capture the horse, and in Lucy, Wildfire brought out feelings of awe and respect. So, one horse—one object—translated many powerful and different emotions into reality; and this animal even made the evil of an outlaw, Cordts, more felt than seen. Cordts appeared only a few times in the book, and even then in an innocuous manner; but Cordts was a horse-thief, and the readers knew almost instinctively that, whereas Bostil probably would not kill for horseflesh, Cordts would. Thus Cordts became one of Grey's most unusual villains because of his prolonged absences in the pages of *Wildfire*. Ordinarily, to keep a major character in a novel subordinated to this extent is the mark of poor technique. When an author can succeed, however, as Grey did, in making a character's influence greater than his presence, the impact is significant.

Grey, perhaps, did not intend for the term "wildfire" to signify anything in particular. Few authors deliberately write symbolism into their own stories. But for this novel, "wildfire" was a horse, it was a condition (Joel Creech's setting the grass afire turned the surroundings into an inferno), and it was a frame of mind. The sacrifice of Wildfire's life set loose the positive events that had been impossible before: the gentle acts of Bostil, and the fulfillment of true love between Lucy and Slone. Thus, sacrifice—on this occasion, a horse's—was made an important key to happiness.

II *Tappan's Burro*

Grey continued to explore man's love of beast, and beast's love of man, in *Tappan's Burro*. This piece of writing, published in 1923 in *Ladies' Home Journal*, was actually a novelette, the main purpose of which was to "glorify the burro." Grey thought several times of enlarging the work to novel length, but he finally decided that its intensity required something shorter than a full-scale book.[3] This decision was a good one on Grey's part because *Ladie's Home Journal* offered him the highest price for the story he had "ever heard of."[4]

Tappan was more a naturalist than a prospector, but mostly he was a dreamer. When he could not leave a newly born, sickly burro to die, he stayed in camp near the Chocolate Mountains in California. During the two weeks he remained at the site, he discovered gold, so he concluded that the burro, whom he named Jenet, had brought him the good luck. As time passed, the man and the animal became inseparable companions. Jenet was Tappan's "ship of the desert," for without her, he could not wander through the wastelands. They camped in the Panamint Mountains on the Northern slope of Death Valley, where Tappan again found gold. Raiders appeared, however, causing Tappan to strike out acrosss Death Valley to elude them. Confronting the terrible furnace winds, Tappan passed into unconsciousness; when a-wakened, he found that Jenet had brought him through the ordeal to an oasis. A grateful Tappan swore that he would never forget Jenet's deed, and together they headed for Superstition Mountain in Arizona where Tappan wanted to search for a gold mine known as The Lost Dutchman.

They did not quite make their destination because of a woman. Tappan and Jenet were camped in the Tonto Country one night when Jake Beam and his sister, Madge, appeared. In due time, Tappan and Madge fell in love with each other, and Madge begged Tappan to take her away from Jake. Tappan agreed, deciding, in the interest of mobility, to leave Jenet behind. On the trail out of the Tonto, Tappan's horses bolted and ran away; while he was tracking them, Madge took his money, and with Jake, who was actually her husband, absconded with it. Tappan spent the next year searching for the Beams. He had no resentment against Madge, just blind love. Then one day he thought of Jenet, so he returned to the Tonto where he found the burro patiently waiting for him. He promised that he would never leave her again. The months turned into years and Tappan began to age. The companionship of Tappan and Jenet became indestructible—not even Madge Beam could have disturbed it.

But another danger threatened the closeness in the form of Jess Blade, who came into Tappan's camp one night claiming that he had been robbed and who was invited by Tappan to share his facilities. When winter arrived, the two men were marooned by a snow storm. Tappan would not leave without Jenet, for heavy snow was the only substance she could not easily traverse. Blade, infuriated, started to shoot Jenet, but Tappan stopped him; and in the fight that followed, Tappan killed Blade. When Tappan attempted to get himself and Jenet out of the snow-bound wilderness, Jenet was dependent on Tappan, for the first time, not only for her well-being but for her very existence. Tappan put Jenet on a folded tarpaulin and pulled her over the crust of the snow, as though on a sled. Far beyond the point where the food vanished, Tappan labored to get out of the snow. He finally made it! Jenet was safe! Tappan could now relax and get a good night's rest. He fell asleep, but he did not awaken the next morning. As a horse had sacrificed his life in *Wildfire* for humans, the opposite was true in *Tappan's Burro*. In both instances, the emphasis was on sacrifice.

As in *Wildfire*, Grey probably had no thought of writing into *Tappan's Burro* any deep psychological insights. All he wanted to do was tell a good story in which the faithfulness of a burro to its master was demonstrated. In the process, however, Grey hit upon some universal themes, which showed the necessity for the emotion of love not only to receive from its object but to bestow itself on the object as well. Tappan had a need to express love toward some other living thing, not especially in a male-female context, but in the form of communion with a creature of nature. This need was the reason Tappan did not hate Madge when she stole his money and left, for she was not that personal to him. Finally, Tappan remembered another object toward which his need to express a love for nature could be satisfied, and thus he returned to Jenet.

Another theme presented by *Tappan's Burro* was familiar to Grey's readers: Tappan wanted to atone for guilt feelings occasioned by his long abandonment of Jenet. The effort to repay his debts and his need for an empathic relationship with a creature of nature caused Tappan to save Jenet from Blade's rifle and then pull the burro over endless miles of snow. It was not love of horseflesh—but more a love for a creature of nature—that made Tappan do these things. He certainly was not the fanatical admirer of horses that Bostil was. Whereas Bostil used horseflesh to gain dominancy over man, Tappan employed it to discover nature itself. His association with Jenet helped him to know that he, too, was a product of nature and was as subject to its rules as any other creature on Earth.

Tappan's Burro magnified emotions that in longer works would not have been so intense. Perhaps this accounted for the story's sustained popularity. Readers could get through it rather quickly and could easily recognize one or more of their own habits in Grey's descriptions and expostulations. This story and *Wildfire* were the only two "horseflesh" works of Grey that had the animals themselves as the prime movers of the plot.[5] In all the others, the horse was central, but people propelled the events.

III   For Love of a Horse

Two such novels were *Forlorn River* (1927) and its sequel, *Nevada* (1928). The setting for the first book was Upper California's Lake Tule area in the late nineteenth century. The principal characters, Ben Ide and "Nevada," were wildhorse hunters who were regarded by many people in neighboring villages as thieves. Ben's one great obsession was to capture the grand wild horse California Red, and his search for the horse produced a number of conflicts.

For one thing, Ben's father was a newly rich rancher who could not understand Ben's "wild" ways of chasing horses. Ben's love was Ina Blaine, daughter of another member of the *nouveau riche*. Ina, who had been to college, was disdainful of the profiteering in land and cattle that she saw about her. "Nevada" loved Hettie Ide, Ben's sister; but, because of "Nevada's" unknown background, Hettie's father forbade any romance. The story's villain was Lew Setter who shrewdly worked through the elder Ide and the elder Blaine to "frame" Ben and "Nevada" as horsethieves. Setter wanted for himself all the land that the two young men had homesteaded; and, in trying to get it, he used the services of a real horse-thief, Bill Hall.

Ben, "Nevada," and an Indian helper named Modoc suspected
Hall of stealing horses on Setter's orders. They tracked Hall one
day, caught him with the incriminating evidence, and besieged
Hall and his men for several weeks. When the outlaw gang had
starved enough, it surrendered; and the whole group headed
back for Tule Lake where Hall promised to confess. On the way,
however, Ben spotted California Red on ice where he could get
little footing so that he could be captured; but it required skill
to bring the great beast under the governance of a rope. When
Ben offered to release Bill Hall and his gang if they would help
capture California Red, Hall agreed; and the job was done. Thus
occurred another episode in which love of horseflesh caused
men's logic to go astray.

After catching California Red, Ben returned to his ranch where
he was attacked by Setter and several cohorts. In the midst of
the fracas, "Nevada" rode up and shot the outlaws. Setter, before
he expired, recognized "Nevada's" true identity; but he was too
weak to divulge it to anyone. "Nevada" left hurriedly, knowing
that he could not remain in the area; for he was really Jim Lacy,
a gunman well known in Nevada. His heart broke as he left his
friend, Ben, and his true-love, Hettie—but such was the doleful
fate of a gunman.

Forlorn River, a 1926 serialization by *Ladies' Home Journal*,
may have been set in the late nineteenth century; but the materialistic, land-grabbing tactics of Setter, Blaine, and Ide were
descriptive of the 1920's. This was a novel, then, in which events
contemporary to Grey figured prominently in thematic development; and the novel presented sharp contrast between old and
young generations. The younger set generally condemned the
new values of profiteering that were creeping into the age; but
both the older men, who had been poor most of their lives, were
rendered irrational by sudden wealth. Grey made it clear that
they were not guilty of evil but of gullibility in letting sharpsters
like Setter manipulate them. "Nevada's" shoot-out at the novel's
end brought all the differing factions together, as Setter and his
henchmen were at last seen in their true light. Ben and his father
were reconciled with each other, and Ben and Ina were married.
The only forlorn characters left were "Nevada" and Hettie, who
longed for each other, and California Red, who simply would not
submit to training techniques and thus remained the wild creature he had always been. There were enough unresolved conflicts
in *Forlorn River* to recommend a sequel; and one appeared as a

serial in late 1926 in *American Magazine* and as a book two years later with the title *Nevada*.

Trouble, in this novel, seemed automatically to follow Jim Lacy, or "Nevada," who was also known now in local circles as "Texas Jack." After fleeing California, he was forced to shoot a man in Lineville, Nevada, an action that caused his hasty departure for Arizona. In that state he became involved with a group of rustlers, the Pine Tree Gang. Cattlemen of the area feared Lacy, but in reality he was a spy for the Cattlemen's Association, his job being to uncover the leader of the outlaw gang.

While these events transpired, the Blaines arrived. They had moved to Arizona for its superior climate after Ben's father had died, and his mother had become ill. Once settled into the cattle-raising business, the Blaine's heard stories about "Texas Jack" and listened to the legends of Jim Lacy. "Nevada" finally succeeded in destroying the head of the rustling outfit, a man who had recently participated in New Mexico's Lincoln County War. Inevitably, Hettie found "Nevada," and very quickly assumed that he was a bad man. All was well, however, when Judge Franklidge, a prominent member of the Cattleman's Association, explained "Nevada's" connection with the outlaws. The Judge gave eloquent testimony not only to Jim Lacy but to the Western gunman in general: "I have met or seen many of the noted killers . . . . These men are not murderers. They are a product of the times. The West could never have been populated without them. They strike a balance between the hordes of ruffians, outlaws, strong evil characters . . . and the wild life of a wild era. It is the West as any Westerner knows it now. And as such we could not be pioneers, we could not progress without this violence . . . . The rub is that only hard iron-nerved youths like Billy the Kid, or Jim Lacy, can meet such men on their own ground" (362). Thus, as in *Riders of the Purple Sage*, Grey showed the significance of the gunman to Western development. Next to his six-shooter, the gunman depended most for his well being on his horse. The gunman and the horse were twin agents of progress in the West.

By the time *Nevada* was published in book form (1928), Grey's long popularity was declining. He had slipped off the best-selling lists in 1925, because, he believed, a new group of writers were getting an increasing amount of *Harper's* attentions and because a continued slump in the book market was caused by radio and movies.[6] Grey felt that his work was not sufficiently publicized:

"In this day of advertizing, *any* author, *any* commodity, no matter how famous or good, must be continually boosted—certainly kept before the public."[7] This condition was somewhat ameliorated for Grey when *Nevada's* popularity got his name listed again in the pages of *The Bookman*.[8] In time, *Nevada* became the best-selling Western of all time,[9] due in part to its copyright expiration, and its going for a time into the public domain. Another reason for its best-selling status was its study of the loner-gunmen and his deeds in producing a civilized West.

IV Wild Horses

The book following *Nevada* continued Grey's fascination with horses. *Wild Horse Mesa*, set in the rugged canyons of Utah in the early 1870's, was published as a book in 1928, but had already been serialized in 1924 by *The Country Gentleman*. Grey wrote most of this book in Long Key, Florida, and he suffered frequent rounds of depression while writing it. When he neared the end of the manuscript of *Wild Horse Mesa*, he worked extraordinarily long periods, writing a minimum of twelve and a maximum of twenty-seven pages a day during the last two weeks of labor.[10]

In this novel, Chayne Weymer with his horse Brutus (one of Grey's horses in real life), hunted for a wild stallion, Panquitch. In doing so, he ran across the Melberne-Loughbridge group whose purpose was to capture and sell wild horses. A sinister figure, Bent Mannerube (in reality, a horse thief), appeared on the scene; and he became in due time foreman for Melberne and Loughbridge. He suggested building enclosures strung with barbed wire into which to drive the horses. This operation was a cruel one, for it killed some horses and injured many. Loughbridge was interested only in profit, however, so he ordered Mannerube to proceed with his plans, causing Melberne to break the partnership. Melberne's decision was helped considerably by the words and deeds of his daughter, Sue, who hated Mannerube and his brutality to horses.

Sue and Chayne disliked, too, Mannerube's treatment of Indians. He was a constant bother to Sosie, an Indian girl who had been educated in white schools and who was, as a result, powerless as a force for social and political advancement. Sosie summed up the problem of trying to go back to tribal life after exposure to white customs: "We girls learn the white people's way of living. We learn to like clean bodies, clean clothes, clean food. When we try to correct our mothers and fathers we're accused of being too good for our own people. My father says to me: 'You're my blood. Why aren't my ways right for you?' Then when I tell him, he can't understand" (29). Ill-treatment of the Indian, so much a part of Zane Grey's literary canon, was a major consideration of *Wild Horse Mesa*; and horses also influenced the action, for love of good horses brought together Chayne Weymer and Toddy Nokin, Sosie's father, and helped them ultimately to defeat the evil designs of Mannerube and his gang.

While chasing horses and protecting Indian rights, Chayne persisted in his search for the wild horse Panquitch. Accompanied by Sue, Chayne spotted the splendid beast one day; and when he trailed him, he led them to a secluded area, full of wild horses, which Chayne immediately named "Wild Horse Mesa." The structure stood as a monument to eternity, and the wild horses on it were nature's handiwork. Chayne exultantly said: "It may be long before another rider, or an Indian, happens on this secret. Maybe never. Some distant day airships might land on Wild Horse Mesa. But what if they do? An hour of curiosity, an achievement to boast of—then gone! Wild Horse Mesa rises even above the world of rock. It was meant for eagles, wild horses—and for lonely souls like mine" (364). The book ended on a note of unity: Melberne and Loughbridge came back together as partners; the effort to capture Panquitch was abandoned, and he remained free to roam his mesa, as much a part of nature as the mesa itself; and Chayne and Sue were married.

The themes of *Wild Horse Mesa* repeated those of dozens of other books Grey wrote. There were many instances in Grey's writings of a cowboy's trailing a wild horse, sometimes for months, catching it, and then turning it loose because of sudden feelings of nobility. When such events occurred, the cowboy seemed to be happier than if he had kept the horse in captivity. By setting the horse free, the cowboy somehow sensed the possessive attitude of nature toward its nobler creatures. Although this situation did not occur in *Wild Horse Mesa*, Chayne's decision to let Panquitch alone was akin to it.

Another thematic concern of *Wild Horse Mesa* was the Indian in relation to the white man. Grey's most famous Indian story was *The Vanishing American*, but he also wrote several short pieces about Indians, including *Blue Feather* (1961) and *The Great Slave* (1920). In dozens of his books, the Indian figured prominently at one point or another. Even when the Indian was obviously wrong, Grey either hinted or stated outright that it was still the white man's fault for bringing out the Indian's savage instincts to begin with. *Wild Horse Mesa* was such a book. Grey's readers expected frequent remarks from him about the ill-treatment of the Indian—not that they intended to do anything about it—and he rarely disappointed them.

Horses offered a livelihood to many citizens of the West and a chance to escape from an unhappy life. This was true for Panhandle Smith, and several other people, in a Grey story serialized by *The Country Gentleman* in 1927 as *Open Range*, and published in book form twenty years later as *Valley of Wild Horses*. The story began in the Texas Panhandle during the height of the cattle industry. Bill Smith called his new-born son Panhandle, over the vigorous protests of his wife, Margaret. In the course of time, Panhandle hit the trail and was separated from his parents for several years. Then he decided one day that a recently developed restlessness was homesickness; thus, he quit his job as a cowpuncher and headed home. When he got there, he found that his parents had departed, the reason being that Bill Smith, who had been cheated out of his property by Jard Hardman, had followed Hardman to New Mexico in hopes of recovering his fortune.

When Panhandle got to Marco, New Mexico, he found his aged and somewhat infirm father who had not recovered his losses from Hardman, and had taken employment in a wagon shop. Upon learning of his family's dire straits, Panhandle stopped Jard Hardman's offensive behavior and also protected his love, Lucy Blake, from the advances of Jard's son Dick. While this fastpaced action occurred, Panhandle discovered a valley full of horses; if they could be captured and sold, the Smith family could earn enough money to realize their dream of homesteading in Arizona. Thus, Panhandle and his father, assisted by several cowboys, set up a wild-horse camp. Unlike so many other wild-horse trappers, Panhandle hated barbed wire and the practice of bending one of the horse's front legs and binding it with leather straps to make it easier to herd the animal.

In discussing the wild-horse camp, Grey gave a useful insight into the spirit of both the cowboy and the horse: "Cowboys were of an infinite variety of types, yet they all fell under two classes: Those who were brutal with horses and those who were gentle. The bronco, the outlaw, the wild horse had to be broken to be ridden. Many of them hated the saddle, the bit, the rider, and would not tolerate them except when mastered. These horses had to be hurt to be subdued. Then there were cowboys, great horsemen, who never wanted any kind of a horse save one that would kick, bite, pitch. It was a kind of cowboy vanity" (123, Pocket Books Ed.).

The Smiths, overcoming the ordeals of adverse weather and bad men, finally gathered enough horses which, when sold at ten dollars a head, enabled them to move to Arizona. Thus, horses offered an opportunity for independence and for the enjoyment of a place that Grey endowed more than once with edenic qualities: Arizona. He once stated that Arizona stars would be moons in any other state.[11] Arizona, first in Grey's ranking of states,[12] became the promised land in *Valley of Wild Horses*, a place dreamed about and yearned for. Only the deserving, Grey made it clear, could benefit permanently from what it had to offer.

V   Horses for Chicken Feed

For the last of his "horse" novels, Grey used a setting in Washington State; but *Horse Heaven Hill* was the worst novel Zane Grey ever wrote. It was kept in manuscript form from the mid-1930's until 1959 when it was published as a book. Grey had little description and philosophy in this book, two attributes of all his other works. The dialogue was especially painful: "If you think I'm wonderful, and if I think you're wonderful, then it must all be wonderful" (63, Black Ed.). There were several interesting episodes in the book; but, on the whole, it was not equal to the rest of Grey's output.[13]

The main activity of the novel was undertaken by Hurd Blanding, who gathered up wild horses at Horse Heaven Hill and sold them for three dollars each to manufacturers of chicken feed. Most of the settlers in the area approved of this gruesome practice because the horses ate the grass reserved for raising cattle. The story's climax was better than the rest of the book foreshadowed, for it gave a vivid description of what happens when men go mad for profit from horseflesh. If the horses were to be sold to chicken-feed manufacturers, there was no special need to keep them healthy. Thus, terrified horses were pushed into small enclosures where they broke their legs and impaled themselves on stakes driven into the fence. In one round-up, over three-thousand horses were shoved into a small corral, where the killing and maiming reached horrendous proportions.

When Grey had finished working on the book, he wrote that "Horse Heaven Hill intrigued me. The idea of killing wild horses for chicken-feed. I was sort of obsessed with the horror of it, to one who loved wild horses."[14] Unfortunately, the story was not convincing, regardless of how true it was. The motive for destroying the horses came at the wrong time; it was just not plausible to sell them for chicken-feed when their value was attested to every day. This misplacement of time and of motive caused many of the novel's events to be forced. Of course, Grey had set other novels in an early period and then moved the plots along with incidents and attitudes that belonged to his own era; a case in point was *Forlorn River*. But in such books, Grey talked about motives that were uniform from the viewpoint of time and place. The failure to do that in *Horse Heaven Hill* produced a poor book.

Perhaps it was fitting that *Horse Heaven Hill* was the last of Grey's "horse" novels. His first one, *Wildfire*, in 1917, was about horses at the height of their splendor; and the mood and style of *Wildfire* matched the conditions of horses it described. *Horse Heaven Hill*, however, showed the once proud horse becoming superannuated, the melancholy fact of which may have affected Grey's writing. During much of the time he wrote the novel, he was traveling. In 1935, he went to Roseburg, Oregon; and in 1936, he visited Australia. On the journeys, he fished, wrote novels and short stories, and took notes for works of the future.[15]

By the early-1930's, Grey no longer feared reviewers. He had written ten years before an extensive "answer to the critics" and had ceased thereafter to let them disturb him. He chose, instead, to pursue the path suggested for him by one of his friends: "I have come to realize the sincerity of Zane Grey, and of his pen, and of the great message he has to deliver. A message of keen appreciation in those things of Nature that are true and clean and beautiful. A sturdy fighting purpose and a steady influence for better understanding of Americanism and of Pioneer days."[16] Above all, Grey wanted to be treated as the sincere author that he was; and he complained about the unfairness of critics in this respect: "I have never yet gotten the kind of criticism that I yearn for. My books do not receive serious reviews. Not one of these higher class critics takes me seriously, if he ever reads me at all . . . . Someday I shall drive past this barren cold coterie of arbiters."[17] He did—several times.

Regardless of Grey's occasional inferior output, he did more to explain the West than any other person contemporary to him. In the 1920's and 1930's, his name was synonymous with a rugged way of life (some journals called him the "high priest of the out-of-doors") and with Western history. Though he no longer occupied the best-selling lists in the 1930's, thousands of readers still followed him faithfully as he explored the themes of unity in nature, greed *versus* benevolence, and the universal might of true love. They believed him when he spoke of the cowboy and his horse because he was an authority.

The subject of horses was, in a way, that of the West itself. It brought out the best and the worst in the people who responded to it. True cowboys loved horses and hated barbed wire. Entrepreneurs loved profit and used barbed wire liberally to get it. Between these two divergent types and views, much Western history occurred. In the long run, the entrepreneur had his way; and the cowboy of the fabulous cattle industry days of the 1880's and 1890's faded into oblivion. Through his novels, however, Grey assured that the cowboy and his faithful horse would not be forgotten. He often reached the heights of ecstasy in his descriptions and memorializations of the American cowboy.

CHAPTER *6*

"Cowboys and Indians"

The open-range cattle industry flourished in the United States approximately between 1865 and 1890. New markets in the East, developed by improved rail facilities, and refrigerated cars, largely accounted for the prosperity. Towns like Abilene and Dodge City, Kansas, became famous because of their location at the junction of a railroad and the "long drive." Thousands of cattle were driven from Texas over a path known usually as the Chisholm Trail, "regardless of where it ran."[1] The "long drive" was lengthy in distance and consuming in time, and its successful operation depended on many things: adequate finances, good weather, pacified Indians, and, most of all, the cowboy's skill. The American cowboy became the most romanticized figure in United States history. His image showed him as an expert marksman, a great lover, an imbiber of strong drink, a practical joker, a protector of womanhood, and a hundred other things. In true life, generally, the cowboy's lot was hard and monotonous, full of strenuous labor. There were enough high points in a cowboy's career, however, to cause writers of fiction to develop the Western story as a distinct genre of literature. Owen Wister set the trend with *The Virginian,* and Zane Grey became its most famous practitioner.

Cowboys were inseparably connected with the open-range cattle industry. In herding cattle for long distances, they developed a jargon and a music peculiarly their own. The cowboys' slow drawl and their ballads (often composed and sung to soothe restless cattle) became famous. Cowboys usually were young and intense, and their long abstentions from gaiety while on the trail caused a number of over-reactions, particularly from drinking "red-liquor," once they got into a town. The dream of practically every cowboy was to have a "spread" of his own. He generally typified a statement made by Benjamin Franklin in the eighteenth century that, until land availability disappeared in America, few people would want to work for somebody else. Therefore, many cowboys yearned to become landlords themselves, and they worked assiduously toward that goal. The cattle industry was conducted by well-established ranchers with the assistance of young men on the way up. Often this arrangement produced cordial relationships between employers and workers, in which not only the virtue of private ownership of property was shown, but chivalric attitudes were demonstrated. Grey elaborated on both of these patterns in his 1939 novel, *Knights of the Range*.

I Comradeship

Knights of the Range was set in Eastern New Mexico in the mid-1870's when the territory had no law except that of the six-shooter. Colonel Lee Ripple, who had come to the area in 1855, had established a huge ranching enterprise on the level of New Mexico's most famous rancher, Lewis Maxwell of Taos. Ripple's daughter, Holly, who took over the ranch after his death, managed its affairs during the most tumultuous time in New Mexico history: "This period saw the inception and development of the Lincoln County War, the bloodiest of all frontier wars [that Grey described], in which three hundred men were killed. It saw the rise of Billy the Kid and Jesse Evans, mere youths in years, but who had not peers in cold nerve, or guncraft, or bloody deeds" (244).

The novel had the usual number of robbers, rustlers, and forlorn lovers. Its distinctive aspect, however, was the "Knights of the Round Table" theme that Grey adopted. Holly, the last of the Ripples, regarded her cowboys not as mere employees but as members of her family. Her father had referred to them as "Rowdies of the Saddle," but Holly changed the title to "Knights of the Range." Every cowboy in her employ loved her; it was clear that they would unhesitatingly die for her. In partial return for this gesture of chivalry toward her, Holly continued her father's tradition of holding an elaborate banquet each year.

At the event in 1874, Holly spoke feelingly to her cowboys, giving an impromptu history of the West, and ending with the serious problems they faced with the area's rustlers. Response to her address was given by Brazos Keene, a Texan, "the wildest, the most untamable, yet the most fascinating and lovable of all Holly's cowboy" (65). After faltering for a moment, Brazos urged his compatriots to ever greater exertions on behalf of their beloved mistress. He even foreswore racial discrimination as he singled out the group's only black cowboy, Ride-em Jackson, and said: "I'm sinkin' race prejudice an' all thet other damn selfish rot. We've got a common cause, men" (151).

Brazos was hopelessly in love with Holly Ripple; but her affections were directed toward a gunman, Renn Frayne, a former Easterner. Frayne led the attack against rustlers and other spoilsmen, while holding to the belief that the line between branding and stealing cattle was difficult to define. The cowboy was the most innocent figure in the matter of appropriating mavericks (unbranded calves roaming the range), yet, said Frayne, he usually got most of the blame. The guilty parties generally were established businessmen who were crooked underneath all of their respectable appearances, and the "McCoy-Slaughter Combine" was an example. Sewall McCoy and Russ Slaughter, as it turned out, were behind the cattle rustling; on the surface, they were respected ranchers. In the climax, when McCoy and Slaughter hired gunman Jeff Rankin to deal with the Knights of the Range, a general shoot-out occurred in which Frayne outdrew Rankin and then also killed McCoy and Slaughter. After this event, Holly and Frayne were married. In despair over losing Holly, Brazos Keene rode away to become a lonely wanderer.

Knights of the Range showed the qualities of loyalty, intemperateness, juvenility, and deadliness characteristic of the American cowboy. It also indicated that some of their mutual concerns were too important to be undermined by long-standing personal beliefs; thus, in the interest of protecting Holly Ripple's property, Brazos Keene gave up his race hatred. A corporate effort in defense of private property was a major idea that Grey developed in *Knights of the Range*, and the welfare of the group was a fitting subject for a novel written during the Depression of the 1930's. Yet Grey had difficulty in selling *Knights of the Range*; for even an old standby of Grey, *Colliers*, turned down the manuscript on grounds that it was too much of a panorama and not enough of story,[2] and *Cosmopolitan* was unable to work out a schedule for it.[3] These rejections showed that an author, no matter how famous he became, still had to convince editors of his work's merits. *Knights of the Range* was finally serialized in 1935 by the *Chicago Tribune*, and it was published in book form in 1939 by Harper's.

A sequel of sorts to *Knights of the Range* was Grey's novel *Twin Sombreros* (1941), which continued the story of Brazos Keene[4] (played by John Wayne in the movie version), the personification of the American cowboy. When the story began, five years had passed since Brazos had left Holly Ripple and Renn Frayne. He had not suffered unduly, however, for he was still very much interested in members of the opposite sex. If he had been a tragic figure like "Hell-Bent Wade" in Grey's *The Mysterious Rider*, Brazos would have rejected womanhood from the viewpoint of personal love. But he was a young cowboy; and heartbreak in young cowboys, Grey demonstrated, was rarely permanent.

The theme of chivalry continued in *Twin Sombreros*, as well as the effort to defend private property from men of ill will. Wandering as he did, Brazos seemed almost automatically to find trouble. He stopped at a cabin one night, for example, and was awakened early the next morning by what he thought was the sound of rain. He smelled blood, however, and he soon discovered a body in the cabin's loft. Naturally, Brazos was "framed" for killing the man, Allen Neece. He was arrested by a crooked deputy sheriff and would have been hanged if a fellow Texan had not interfered immediately.

After exoneration for the Neece murder, Brazos decided to find out who the culprits were. He visited Abe Neece, Allen's father, and discovered that Neece was once the owner of a ranch called "Twin Sombreros," now in the hands of a dubious character, Raines Surface. Another discovery, more pleasant than the first, was identical twins, June and Janis, daughters of Abe Neece; for Brazos quickly fell in love with both girls. In due time, Brazos discovered that Surface was behind the Neece killing and that he had wrongly taken the elder Neece's ranch. After restoring the ranch to Neece, Brazos faced another difficulty: which twin did he want, and how could he tell them apart? One solution to the problem was that he marry both of them. Being fearful of polygamy, however, Brazos again hit the trail. He was followed and found in a Texas town by Janis Neece; the two were wed, the book ended.

Twin Sombreros, serialized in 1940 by the *New York News Syndicate* and published as a book the following year, emphasized the doctrine of good works. Brazos Keene was only one of hundreds of men roaming the Western regions, deliberately playing the role of the Good Samaritan—playing it, in the case of Brazos, to forget the supposed heartbreak of losing Holly Ripple. The book was not so realistic nor so historically significant, in Grey's opinion, as several of his other productions; but he predicted success for it.[5] However, the magazine to which he first submitted it, *Collier's*, turned it down. In assessing his publishing problems in the mid-1930's, Dolly advised Grey to write "one of your old-time exciting stories."[6] She also urged him to readapt himself to present conditions. Dolly told him: "It is only age that cannot change, and you are not old. You have the youth and flexibility still to conquer, but you have fallen into ways of self-indulgence, into vanities of position." Dolly then gave a glimpse of the effects of the Depression: "Believe me, no one is too proud to retrench in these days. It is those who do not when they ought to, who are looked down upon."[7] Such counsel from Dolly indicated that she was the strongest single force in Zane Grey's life.

Somewhat similar to *Knights of the Range* and *Twin Sombreros* in themes of chivalry, but not so fully executed, was Grey's novel, *Raiders of Spanish Peaks* (1938), originally titled, *The Three Range Riders*.[8] Three men, Laramie Nelson, Trace Williams, and Lonesome Mulhall, became famous throughout Kansas and a part of Colorado as shooters, trackers, and lovers. Their major objective was to save enough money to buy a ranch, so at the basis of all their escapades was the desire to own property. One day the trio rode into Garden City, Kansas, founded by "Buffalo" Jones, the man with whom Grey first went West. In the town, they met Jones and a friend of his, John Lindsay of Sandusky, Ohio. Lindsay had bought a ranch in Colorado called "Spanish Peaks." He was such a tenderfoot that Jones easily talked Nelson, Mulhall, and Williams into accompanying Lindsay to Colorado and getting him started as a rancher. Lindsay's three beautiful daughters helped the cowboys considerably in making their decisions. Thus the stage was set for what to Zane Grey readers was an ordinary Western situation: strong, manly Westerners helping weak, effete Easterners get a new start in life. This assistance seemed to be the mission of those who had grown up in the West; and rarely did their goodwill, practiced in splendid settings, fail to transform the Easterner.

Rustling, claimed Grey, was the biggest problem of ranchers during the last quarter of the nineteenth century. "Buffalo" Jones told Lindsay what was ahead of him:

We are now in the midst of what I might call the third great movement of early frontier history—the cattle movement. . . . For years now vast herds of cattle have been driven up out of Texas to Abilene and Dodge, the cattle terminus. From these points cattle have been driven North an' West an' shipped East on cattle-trains. The cattle business is well on an' fortunes are bein' made. With endless range, fine grass an' water, nothin' else could be expected. . . . But rustlin' now is a business. The rustler has come into his own. He steals herds of cattle in a raid. Or he will be your neighbor rancher, brandin' all your calves. The demand for cattle is big. Ready money always. An' this rustlin' is goin' to grow an' have its way for I don't know how long. Years, anyway (59).

Jones's speech to Lindsay laid the framework for most of the story. The three cowboys fought off rustlers and other intruders while the Colorado air restored the elder Lindsay to health and the setting made a man of his son. During this process, fully predictable love affairs blossomed between the cowboys and the three Lindsay girls. The rustlers were routed or hanged, a Cattleman's Protective Association was formed, and love reigned supreme on Spanish Peaks Ranch. The story was typically Grey because of its themes—the transforming qualities of the West, Western chivalry, defending private property—and because of its descriptions of cowboys. There was little difference in the personality of a cowboy who fought for "law and order" and one who rustled cattle. The same type of humor (usually in the form of practical jokes) characterized both persons, and the same inclinations toward the fair sex were paramount. The difference, then, between violent men who are good and violent men who are bad, Grey indicated, was indeed minute.

This concept was pursued in Grey's novel, *Arizona Ames*, serialized in 1929 by *McCall's*, and published in 1932 as a book. Rich Ames, from the Tonto Country, knew the ways of violence; but he never used them for ill until he shot three men, one of whom had despoiled his sister. The deed necessitated Rich's flight from Arizona and doomed him to a life of wandering under the name of "Arizona Ames." Rich became the "Don Quixote" of the West as he roamed from place to place helping needy people, mostly females. He shot Crowe Grieve for mistreating his wife and for being, in general, a rotten human being. When Rich went to Utah, he protected a Mormon from the overbearing tactics of bad men; and he finally wandered into Colorado where he met Ester Halstead, fell in love with her, and accordingly planned to give up his travelings.

Arizona Ames, said Grey, "was a typical character of his period. Every range from the Pan Handle to the Black Hills, and as far West as the Pecos, had its Ames." He fit admirably the role of the cowboy: "He [the cowboy] came from the four corners of the United States, and beyond. At most he was a boy not yet out of his teens; but then life of the range, the toil and endurance demanded by cattle-raising, the border saloon, the gambling-hell, the rustler, developed him at once into a man, and one that eventually made the West habitable" (98).

II Black Cowboys

In addition to depicting the stereotype cowboy in his novels, Grey also discussed some of the thousands of black cowboys who journeyed throughout the Western regions. A recent book said of the black cowboy: "Now they are forgotten, but once they rode all the trails, driving millions of cattle before them. . . . They numbered thousands, among them many of the best riders, ropers and wranglers."9 Usually, books about the West, both fiction and nonfiction, neglected the black man's contributions to Western settlement—indeed, even his presence. Grey wrote about black cowboys in several of his books but in three in particular.

In *Knights of the Range* (1939), Ride-em Jackson was a highly respected person. He was asked once to give testimony against a white man, a procedure practically non-existent in that country at the time. His riding abilities were unmatched in New Mexico territory, and his fame in this respect spread far and wide. On a bet with Russ Slaughter, Jackson broke the toughest bronc in the area: "He appeared to wrap himself around the horse and to bend flat, almost to the ground. . . . On the instant, with a horrid scream the horse raised himself spasmodically with a cracking of hoofs. Like a burr Jackson's body appeared stuck upon him. . . . He had sunk his teeth in the nose of the horse, which made it impossible for the animal to get its head. And when they came up together the horse had his head high, turned back in a distorted way, with the little Negro like a leech upon his neck" (186-87). While the champion rider of the outfit, Ride-em Jackson, along with Brazos Keene, was also a great practical joker. On Holly Ripple's wedding day Jackson went to her and said in all seriousness that Frayne had just gone after rustlers and had no time to marry her. She believed him until she saw the other cowboys snickering at her discomfort.

Raiders of Spanish Peaks (1938) featured a black vaquero who was part of a rustling outfit headed by Lester Allen, the man from whom John Lindsay bought Spanish Peaks Ranch. (Here was another instance of a rancher, respectable on the surface, conducting a huge illicit cattle business—see p. 102.) The black man, Sam

Johnson, was finally induced to incriminate Allen in the rustling operations; and his testimony was the key to breaking the rustling ring.

A third Grey novel with a black cowboy as a major character was *West of the Pecos* (1937). Sambo Jackson, whose reputation was well known west of the Pecos River, had accompanied his former master, Colonel Templeton Lambeth, to the area from East Texas just after the Civil War. Sambo became the protector of the Colonel's daughter, Terrill, after the Colonel died. (The Colonel had wanted a boy when Terrill was born, so he gave her a boy's name, dressed her like a boy, and taught her to act like a boy.) Sambo was the only person in the town of Eagle's Nest who knew that Terrill Lambeth was really a girl. The main white character of the novel, Pecos Smith, soon learned to respect Sambo Jackson: "Pecos Smith had known Negro slaves as worthy as any white man, though he had the Southerner's contempt for most of the black trash. This man, Sambo, had the build of a vaquero, and Pecos remembered him. His boots and spurs gave further proof to Pecos" (97).

The chief theme of *West of the Pecos* dealt with the nuances of cattle rustling and appropriations of mavericks. Many cowboys, including Pecos Smith, got their start as ranchers in this way, although an unwritten law of the range dictated that, before a man could take mavericks, he had to be a rancher. Thus, for a non-rancher to brand mavericks was clearly a case of rustling. At the end of the book Pecos Smith and Sambo Jackson broke the rustling ring in the area. Pecos discovered that Terrill Lambeth was really a girl, he married her, and became a powerful and respected rancher.

Grey sold *West of the Pecos* to *American Magazine*, where it was serialized in 1931 but not before revisions were made. Originally, Grey had given the story two unrelated beginnings, one dealing with Colonel Lambeth's journey from East Texas and the other with Pecos Smith's branding of mavericks. For a magazine serialization, the story initially lacked the necessary unity,[10] so the Colonel's trip was to a large extent edited from the final version.

There were several other instances in Grey's books of black cowboys herding, singing, and cooking to keep the cattle drives moving and the ranches working. Although Grey was primarily interested in the Indian's minority status, he by no means overlooked the contributions of the blacks to Western development.

III Mavericks

On the matter of dealing with mavericks, Grey elaborated fully in his novel, *The Maverick Queen* (1950). Kit Bandon of Wyoming's Wind River Mountain area bought maverick calves from rustlers, and such purchases provided the foundation for a growing dispute between cowboys and cattlemen which ultimately produced a range war. Into the midst of these growing difficulties came Lincoln Bradway from Nebraska to investigate the mysterious death of his friend, Jimmy Weston. Before the book ended, it was clear that Jimmy had been caught appropriating mavericks and had been hanged by cattlemen: "Lincoln had heard that the ranchers of Western Wyoming, hoping to induce rustlers to give their ranges a wide berth, had adopted the ruthless practice of hanging a cattle thief without formality" (4).

Lincoln's desire to destroy Kit's operation was tempered by his affection for Kit's niece, Lucy. This love affair infuriated Kit, who wanted Lincoln for herself. She threw temper tantrums when she discovered that Lincoln was one man she could not manipulate. Finally, however, Kit was captured by a group of cattlemen and unceremoniously hanged, thereby showing the terribly direct justice of the frontier and indicating that womanhood, respected as it was in the West, still had to maintain certain codes of conduct or suffer the consequences. When the book ended, Lincoln had turned Wyoming itself into the major character: "He [Lincoln] had come to avenge a crime and had found his true mate here in these hills. He knew that this love of Wyoming was permanent and ineradicable and that somewhere under the shadow of these peaks he would make his home" (155-56). Again, Grey allowed setting to triumph over characterization; for *The Maverick Queen* depicted the cruelty of frontier days. If any proverb could effectively describe the theme of this novel, it would be: "Pride goeth before a fall." Kit Bandon was full of vanity and arrogance during the time she was the "maverick queen," and these very characteristics, as well as her deeds led her straight to the gallows.[11]

IV A Rustling Preventive

One way of controlling rustling was to use a drift fence, a barbed wire structure built so that cattle could be controlled in their grazing. Though often illegal because it crossed open range or private property, it was a way for ranchers to keep a close watch on their cattle, and it provided an easy patrol area. Drift fences, however, were unpopular with cowboys because of the barbed wire. Moreover, the people in areas where the cattle were prevented from wandering regarded drift fences as affronts to their honesty. Nonetheless, many ranchers resorted to drift fences to keep their cattle from straying and thus being rustled. Grey wrote of such an event in his novel, *The Drift Fence* (1933).

The book described the effects of suddenly thrusting a tenderfoot into the role of a foreman who had to supervise a wild group of cowboys. When Jim Traft from Missouri arrived in Arizona at his uncle's invitation to head the Diamond Ranch outfit in the Tonto region, the tenderfoot's first decision was to build a drift fence one hundred miles long to solve the rustling problem. Many cowboys balked at the idea, and only through perseverance and fistfights did Jim Traft have his way. While constructing the fence, the cowboys, trying to force him to give up the project, played all kinds of practical jokes on Traft.

Traft met and fell in love with Molly Dunn of the Cibeque, an area isolated by the drift fence. Traft's and Molly's initial hostility because of the fence was soon overcome, but trouble persisted between Traft and Molly's brother, "Slinger," a gunman. When they fought, "Slinger" tried to "rooster" Traft by fighting on his back and swinging his spurs at his antagonist. Traft won the fight, however, and also "Slinger's" respect. If there was anything that a true Westerner liked, it was fortitude and bravery, especially in someone who was not a native Westerner. After the event, "Slinger" helped the Diamond Ranch group; and, by the time winter stopped the building, sixty of the planned one hundred miles of the drift fence were constructed.

The Drift Fence, serialized in 1929 by *American Magazine* and published in 1933 as a book regained for Grey some of his popularity among readers of America because it gave excellent glimpses of what cowboy life was really like. Perhaps the realism in this respect came from Grey's own personal experiences in living with cowboys. He knew their ways, and also their tricks, and he became fond of practical joking, the trademark of the American cowboy. Grey knew he had a winner with *The Drift Fence*, even while writing it. It took him only fifty-seven days to write the original manuscript of 466 pages. He never missed a day of working on it, rising each morning at five and working for two hours. The early morning labor was a real revelation to him: he felt it was "some stunt. If the novel is good I sure have discovered something."[12]

One of the obstacles in building the drift fence was a gang of outlaws known as the "Hash Knife," and Grey wrote of this group in a sequel to *The Drift Fence*: *The Hash Knife Outfit*. The novel was so entitled because these outlaws always left their "calling-card" after a job—a picture of a hash knife, though its original title had been *The Yellow Jacket Feud*. In the novel, the plot was generated by the competition over ownership and operation of the Yellow Jacket Ranch. Jed Stone, a leader of the Hash Knife outfit, had mellowed in his ways; he wanted to give up his wild life, but a member of his gang, Croak Malloy, would not let him. Finally, after Stone had shot the scoundrel, he turned his attention to a traditional Western practice: the "saving" of Jim Traft's sister, Gloriana, who had come to Arizona. Jed made Gloriana believe that all sorts of dreadful things were about to happen to her, causing her to turn away from her characteristic petulance. Her experience helped her accept a cowboy's offer of marriage; thus another successful Zane Grey romance was placed before readers eager to read it.[13]

V The Long Drive

Grey's study of the American cowboy extended far beyond the ranch and the range, for an important aspect of the cowboy's life was the long drive from the range to the rail head. Life on the trail was vigorous, requiring immense amounts of stamina; indeed, the work on the trail, rather than on the ranch or on the range, ultimately produced for most people the image of the cowboy. On the trail cowboys sang ballads, told tall tales, imagined fantasies of wealth and faraway places, and dreamed of home and sweethearts. Their life on the trail turned the cowboy into an American institution which endeared itself to millions of people. To an extent, all of Grey's cowboy novels featured the trail; but two were specifically about the long drive.

Although *Wilderness Trek* (1944) was set in Australia, its characters and events were typically American. The central figures of the novel, Sterling Hazelton and Red Krehl, were former Arizona cowboys who had left the United States because of problems with love and law. In Australia, they agreed to lead a huge herd of cattle across the continent, a feat that required two years of as strenuous an existence as it was possible for man to have. On the trail, race hatred occurred when Ashley Ormiston mistreated the aborigines; peril stalked the way as the group had to cross several crocodile-infested rivers; unbearable heat and hordes of flies accompanied the group; but there was, finally, the one thing that made the trip worthwhile: love. This book, like so many others of Grey's novels, ended in a double wedding.

Grey had first visited Australia in the mid-1920's to fish for swordfish, tuna, and anything else he could catch. Impressed with Australia's likeness to America in regard to cattle raising and the long drives, he thought for years of writing a novel with an Australian setting; but he did not accomplish his goal until 1936; but the novel was not published by Harper's until 1944. A letter from Dolly predicted the book's future popularity: "It is really remarkable that you have achieved so much popularity in Australia—or perhaps it is not so remarkable at all. You are doing a great deal to put Aurstralia on the map in a sporting way and I am glad they appreciate it . . . . I think the Australian cowboy idea might go over pretty well in this country."[14] Though Grey had earlier angered some New Zealanders and Australians for casting aspersions on their fishing methods, he continued to be a "household" word in those areas. One of his favored remembrances was seeing in New Zealand a ship named after one of his novels, *Desert Gold*.

A book that put Grey briefly on the best-selling lists again was *The Trail Driver* (serialized by *McCall's* in 1931; published by Harper's in 1936), the story of a cattle drive which suffered numerous hardships from rustlers, electric storms, stampedes, floods, doublecrossings, and Indian attacks. Only the strongest could survive these ordeals along the Chisholm Trail. In the words of one of the book's characters, Adam Brite, the cattle drives represented the "swing of Texas toward an Empire." The cattle industry became so significant that thousands of Easterners eagerly invested their money in the enterprise.[15] The movement, Brite believed, was "singular" and "tremendous," providing a way for Texans to restore themselves to economic solvency.

The Trail Driver was typical of Grey's writing for its romances, mistaken identities, and overheard conversations. It gave a vivid description of Dodge City, Kansas: "On the wide sidewalk a throng of booted, belted, spurred men wended their way up or down. The saloons roared. Black-sombreroed, pale-faced, tight-lipped men stood beside the wide portals of the gaming-dens. Beautiful wrecks of womanhood, girls with havoc in their faces and the look of birds of prey in their eyes, waited in bare-armed splendor to be accosted. Laughter without mirth ran down the walk. The stores were full. Cowboys in twos and threes and sixes trooped by, young, lithe, keen of eye, bold of aspect, gay and reckless" (300).

VI The Gunman

Grey also discussed the gunman in *The Trail Driver*, as he had in several other novels: "The gunman sought the dramatic, took advantage of the element of surprise, subjected no other to risk [except, of course, his opponent] than himself" (145). The Western gunman was the strongest drawn character in all the Zane Grey novels, and characters like Lassiter of *Riders of the Purple Sage* and Jim Lacey of *Forlorn River* and *Nevada* were more believable than most of Grey's other characters. Competition as a way of life in the West was a historical fact, making it reasonable to expect a gunman's reputation to be constantly challenged. To keep himself alive, the gunman had to become ever more adept at his deadly act. Most gunmen were cowboys of whom their home communities were proud; this type of gunman killed only when he had to. On the other hand, fastdraw artists in the West were often "sheriffs with an itch to kill instead of arrest, cowboys on the rampage, gamblers who shot to hide their cheating" (*The Lone Star Ranger*, 12). There were also gunmen whose status as either outlaw or peaceful citizen was uncertain, and gunmen who had repented of their deeds but had to suffer the consequences.

In *The Lone Star Ranger* (1915), Grey showed the stages of creating a gunman; and the novel[16] was valuable for its psychological insights into a gunman. It was also pessimistic, hinting broadly that Buck Duane, the central character, whose father had been a gunman, really did not have a choice in the matter; that some chromosome factor dictated that he be a gunman.

When Cal Bain forced Buck to draw, Buck's victory in the shoot-out caused him to acquire an instant reputation. He hit the trail, for Texas Rangers were warring on gunmen at the time (1870's) because they were trying to eliminate the shoot-out as a way of settling arguments. Therefore, a gunman was regarded by the Rangers as a criminal, no matter how pure of heart he was. The gunman's life was a haunted, and, lonely one: he was always blamed for crimes whether he committed them or not; his victims constantly came back to haunt him; as he sat before campfires and as he tried to sleep at night, "Every one of his victims, singly and collectively, returned to him for ever, it seemed, in cold, passionless, accusing domination of these haunted hours. They did not accuse him of dishonor or cowardice or brutality or murder; they only accused him of death" (116). In time, he accepted the dictum: "A gunfighter has to kill a man to forget the last victim." Thus, his lot was one of unceasing situations in which he must kill or be killed.

Buck Duane was one of the lucky gunmen; for Captain NcNelly of the Rangers, who had been chasing Duane, offered a pardon in return for Buck's help in capturing the illusive outlaw Chisildine, an offer that Buck quickly accepted. He traveled to the Texas area West of the Pecos where he came into contact with Granger Longstreth who had a beautiful daughter, Ray. Ultimately, Buck discovered that Longstreth was behind the outlaw operations, so he faced a dilemma: how to expose Longstreth (Buck suspected he was Chisildine) and love his daughter at the same time. This conflict was solved when Buck's and Ray's love for each other became so intense that Longstreth quit his illegal life and returned to his native Louisiana and when Buck discovered that Floyd Lawson was actually Chisildine.

After the outlaw leaders had been dispersed, either by train or by bullet, Duane's job was ended; but he decided to confront Poggin. Ray Longstreth remonstrated against him for still wanting gunplay, and Zane Grey explained why Buck wanted to meet Poggin: "His father's blood, that dark and fierce strain, his mother's spirit, that strong and unquenchable spirit of the surviving pioneer—these had been in him; and the killings, one after another, the wild and haunted years, had made him, absolutely in spite of his will, the gunman. . . . Actual pride of his record! Actual vanity in his speed with a gun! Actual jealousy of any rival!" (294-95). The two gunmen were roughly comparable in their talents. Poggin shot Buck five times; but, when Buck awakened, he learned that Poggin was killed.

Buck Duane's career as a ranger and (hopefully) as a gunman ended with his marriage to Ray Longstreth and their departure for Louisiana, for Buck wanted to go where his reputation was not known; in the West, however, to find such an area was virtually impossible. The problem for Duane was how to escape the stigma of the past and to lead an ordinary, peaceful life. In most instances, the man who tried to accomplish such a feat was doomed to disappointment.

An exception to this rule, however, was discussed by Grey in *Shadow on the Trail*, which was published in 1946 seven years after Grey's death. Grey was inspired to write the novel by the experiences of Sam Bass and his outlaws. One day in the 1870's in Mercer, Texas, Bass and his gang were ambushed while robbing the town's bank; and only one robber escaped. Grey wondered about former outlaws—about what they had done and how they had lived after they had relinquished their careers of crime. He said in the book's foreword: "It is within the province of the creative writer to take upon himself the task of imagining and portraying what might have happened to one of these vanishing outlaws. And that is what I have tried to do in *Shadow on the Trail*."

The first objective of Wade Holden when the gang was ambushed was to elude the Texas Rangers who were led by Captain Mahaffey whose motto was "run the man down." Fortuitously, Holden found in a prairie-schooner encampment a sympathetic female, Jacqueline Pencarrow, who hid him in her tent while Mahaffey was in the area. Then, predictably, the novel shifted forward several years to a setting in Arizona where Holden discovered the Pencarrow family. The father had tried ranching for some time, only to be intimidated by the area's bad men. Holden put himself at Pencarrow's service, cleaned out the outlaws and rustlers (earning a highly respected reputation as a gunman), and fell in love with Jacqueline. In time, the two were married; and happy years passed, during which the Holdens became proud parents. Wade was just on the verge of forgetting his associations with outlaws, when Captain Mahaffey one day appeared. But Mahaffey was impressed with Wade's present condition; for what a man becomes rather than what he had been was an important consideration in Mahaffey's thinking. Therefore, his visit turned out to be only social.

Shadow on the Trail showed conclusively that "violence is violence," whether it is committed by good men or bad; for Wade Holden did not give up violence but merely changed sides. The number of casualties he inflicted while on the side of "good" was as high, or higher, as when he had belonged to the "bad." Grey's book did not live up to the promise that its beginning set for it; for the novel missed its chance at greatness by treating in an ordinary way themes of potentially intense poignancy. If the attitude and thought of a reformed outlaw had been emphasized instead of allowing "business as usual," except in a different location and for a new clientele, the book would have been more powerful than it was.[17]

Grey's life-long study of the American cowboy dealt mostly with chivalry, ownership of property, rustling, black cowboys, mavericks, the long drive, the gunman, cowboy humor, and the loner. In his "apologia" to the critics in the mid-1920's Grey summarized his feelings toward the cowboy: "The poor cowboy! Who is there to save him from oblivion? The cheap novel, the

modern movie, have almost blotted him from history. But he
was heroic. More than the frontiersman, the soldiers, the pioneers, the American cowboy opened the West for civilization.
. . . Who could exaggerate the ordeal of the cowboy?"[18] Grey
blended the cowboy's attributes into the cattle industry, and
thus described a fantastic era in American history. The cowboy took, however, a proprietary view of the Western regions—
an attitude that made inevitable trouble and war with the Indians.
Two tribes of South Plains Indians in particular, the Kiowas and
the Comanches, confronted the cowboy's advance; and Grey
wrote two lengthy novels that dealt with these encounters.

VII Cowboys Versus Indians

In *Fighting Caravans* (originally titled *The Overland Freighter*[19]
set in the 1870's, and first published in 1928 by *Country Gentleman*), the characterization of the hero and the heroine was
treated in a typically Grey manner, but the book was valuable
for its geographical and historical descriptions. Clint "Buff"
Belmet and May Bell, both mere babes, promised fidelity to each
other as they traveled West with their parents. "Buff" Belmet became an overland freight hauler after Indians had killed his
mother and father and had kidnapped his sweetheart, May Bell.
"Buff" carried furs, pelts, and buffalo hides along the Old Trail,
which ran from Kansas to New Mexico. He had earlier sympathized
with the Indians, but was now determined to be an Indian killer
after the slaying of his parents and the kidnapping of his true-
love. The Kiowa Indian chieftain, Satock, was a constant menace
to the caravans; but the most dangerous Indians were the Comanches led by Nigger-Horse. Not even the wagon trains' cannons
could stop the Comanches when they were on the rampage. (It
was rare for a wagon train to possess a cannon.)

One gruesome episode after another occurred as Clint ("Buff")
drove his wagon trains between Kansas and New Mexico, and
"Buff's" reputation as a freighter and Indian fighter spread rapidly. He was hailed everywhere, but at heart he was a lonely man,
lamenting the loss of May Bell. Through his travels, "Buff" met
such prominent frontiersmen as Dick Curtis and Kit Carson, as
well as the most famous rancher in New Mexico territory, Lewis
Maxwell of Taos. Maxwell, a friend of the Indians, sold beef to
the United States Army—a most profitable enterprise during the
Civil War. When Maxwell urged "Buff" to stop being a hauler
and to settle down because the West needed permanent citizens,

"Buff" could not do so because he had to find May. After a huge Indian offensive, in concert with white renegades led by Charley Bent (the Simon Girty of the Plains), he finally found her. May had believed all these years that "Buff" was dead. Their reunion ended *Fighting Caravans* on a poignant note.

Related to *Fighting Caravans* because of its descriptions of cowboy-Indian confrontation, was another Grey novel, *The Lost Wagon Train* (1936). The main character, Stephen Latch, a Southerner, was attending college in the North when the Civil War erupted. When his failure to obtain a commission in the Confederate Army embittered him, he went to the West where he planned to rob wagon trains. He formed a partnership with Satana, Chief of the Kiowas. (The other Kiowa Chief, Satock, stopped his operations in 1863.) Satana and his men had plenty of rum to fortify themselves for the job at hand. After attacking the trains, the Indians killed everybody and rolled the wagons over a cliff so they could not be found. At first, Latch was conscience-stricken because of all the murders; but he turned his heart to steel. He had been wronged by the world, he felt, and he intended to strike back.

On the very first wagon train, Latch discovered that his old sweetheart, Cynthia Bowden, was a passenger; and he saved her from the Indians and later married her. They lived in Spider Web Canyon in New Mexico where Cynthia knew little of Latch's activities. Latch took possession of a wide area that he called "Latch's Field," upon which he wanted to build a ranch that would rival Maxwell's in hospitality. When he heard that his wife had died giving birth to a child, Latch left the place without visiting the scene of birth and without learning that he had a daughter. When he returned six years later, he found his little girl, Estelle, who had been cared for in his absence by friends.

Latch gave up his business of massacring the occupants of wagon trains, for his one objective now was to keep his beloved daughter from learning about his dreadful past. There were people, however, like Leighton, Latch's former partner, who held Latch's past as a "hammer" over his head. A fierce climax occurred when Leighton captured Latch, took him to the canyon where the ruined wagon trains were located, made him sign over his ranch to Leighton, and told him that Estelle was being brought to the scene to hear the truth about her father's past.

An observer of these events, "Slim Blue" (who was really the brother of Lester Cornwall, one of Latch's early comrades) was hidden in underbrush, and he intended to save Latch from Leighton. Before this happened, however, Latch worked free and ripped Leighton apart with his knife. Blue then came out into the open and viewed the ghastly scene: "Faces of rugged pioneers, scalped heads of women, nude bodies of children gazed mournfully . . . upon Blue [though, apparently, the massacres had occurred long ago]. . . . He had seen the work of Satana and Latch. Bloody devils! He ground his teeth in irrepressible rage. But the fierce Kiowa chief could be understood, for the white man had driven him into the waste places, robbed him of meat. But not so Latch! What a monster" (374). Even so, Blue married Latch's daughter, Estelle, and moved to Boston with her so that Latch's secret would be kept from her. This was the only book Grey ever wrote in which going East from the West had a beneficial effect, and in which a major villain was not legally punished for his crimes.

Grey wrote much of *The Lost Wagon Train* in early 1931 while on the way to Tahiti. He must have been in a bloody frame of mind, for *Collier's* changed the manuscript on the grounds that the massacre conspiracy between Latch and Satana was so utterly cruel that readers would be unpleasantly affected.[20] The book, however, incorporated all of the gruesome events.

Fighting Caravans and *The Lost Wagon Train* were historical studies, hinting broadly at the inevitability of conflict between the red and white man. Grey again made it clear that the white man was basically responsible for the confrontation. The books were valuable, too, for their descriptions of caravan trails such as the different routes of the Old Trail: Mountain and Middle, along the Cimarron River to Santa Fe, and *Journado del Muerta* (Journey of Death) across the desert. Grey noted the effects of the Civil War and its aftermath on the Southwestern regions as he described the multitudes of Northerners and Southerners who poured into the area to start their lives anew. Such migrations produced a frenzied time, indeed. The books showed, also, the once proud Redman reduced to a level of bestiality. Elsewhere in Grey's writing, he stated that the freighter era was the first great movement of frontier history (the periods of the buffalo hunter and cattle industry being the next two) because it laid the foundation for the cowboy-Indian hostilities.

VIII Other Indian Stories

Grey wrote several short stories dealing specifically with habits, customs, and activities of various Indians; but his best story was "The Great Slave," which was about a Crow named Siena to

whom a "shooting stick" was a symbol of salvation. Siena used the
instrument at first to kill elk and moose for food; and later he
freed his tribe from slavery with the gun. The story was ironic because the "shooting-iron," so valuable to Siena and his tribe, ultimately figured most prominently in destroying Indian power.
Another short story that dealt with racism, vengeance, and the
terrific differences between slavery and freedom was "Yaqui."
The Yaquis and the Mexicans were sworn foes, and neither received mercy at the hands of the other.[21]

Still another short story was "Blue Feather," which concerned
ancient groups of Indians known as the Nopahs (the name Grey
gave to the Indians in his novel, *The Vanishing American*) and
the Sheboyahs. Blue Feather, from the Nopahs, was sent into the
Sheboyah camp to undermine their culture to make invasion possible and easy. He did not count on meeting the beautiful maid-
en, Nashta; he fell so deeply in love with her that he lied to his
father, Nothis Tah, about the strength of the Sheboyahs, saying
that their cliff dwellings were worthless. When Nothis Tah attacked and discovered Blue Feather's prevarications about Sheboyah strength, he wanted to execute him. Love won the day,
however, when Nashta successfully begged for Blue Feather's
life. Nothis Tah contented himself with setting aside a day on
which a large number of "little people" (the Sheboyahs) would be
thrown off cliffs. Thus was born a traditional celebration (for
everybody, that is, but the Sheboyahs) in honor of the Nopah
victory over their enemies.

Grey had the greatest sympathy for the Indian, and he constantly lamented the government's mistreatment of them. Grey
regarded the broken treaties and the reservation system as shame-
ful—a dark blotch on the pages of United States history. Certainly, he did not condone the Indian's violence; but, in appor-
tioning blame for violence in general, Grey argued that the onus
rested on the white man's shoulders. All the way from *Betty Zane*,
written in 1903, to *The Lost Wagon Train*, published in 1936,
Grey defended the rights of the American Indian.

Grey truly loved the American cowboy, both the historical
ones and those contemporary to him. He deeply respected American Indians because he sincerely believed they had been wronged
and because Indian blood flowed in his own veins. The two
forces—cowboys and Indians—competed against each other, the
cowboys foraging an empire, the Indians fighting for survival.
Grey became the leading chronicler of the hostilities engineered
by these varying objectives.

IX *Grey's Modern Cowboys*

Although Grey usually discussed only those cowboys who had passed into history, he in one instance wrote *The Code of the West* (1934), a major novel about the effects of automobiles and other equipment, as well as modern thinking, on the American cowboy.[22] *The Code of the West* emphasized, too, the cowboy in a setting of change—a not unusual thing for Grey to do; for he had employed this theme in other novels such as *The Light of Western Stars*. The automobile changed the lives of most cowboys in the 1920's. Usually, cowboys drove cars as though they were breaking broncs. In general, the car was viewed with suspicion by cowboys and by Grey personally; for automobiles, which made noise, disrupted the normal flow of events for nature's creatures. Thus, the motor, an unnatural thing thrust into natural surroundings, was entirely out of place.

The novel struck a familiar chord among Grey readers because it condemned the "new morality" that had crept into the American system after World War I. After Mary Stockwell, a teacher, had arrived in the Tonto Basin in Arizona, her seventeen-year-old sister, Gloriana, joined her. Gloriana, a "flapper" type, was much interested in the "liberation" of the American woman. Even when Gloriana was at her rebellious worst, however, the reader knew instinctively that the West would ultimately conquer her. The West's openness, its naturalness, "the simplicity of its people," the "necessity for development of physical strength," and the code of cowboy Cal Thurman, worked its magic on the spoiled young girl from the East.

When Cal Thurman forcibly took Gloriana and married her, he told himself he did so to protect Gloriana from herself. If she were married, scoundrels like Bid Hatfield would stop making advances toward her, and she would be freed from so much temptation. Cal's deed was the ultimate step in the "code": it was easy to beat up a man under the "code," perhaps even to kill, but to marry someone in tribute to the "code" was magnanimous indeed. As it turned out, however, Cal really loved Gloriana; and she really loved him. It was not the love, though, that counted so far as the "code" was concerned; it was Cal's willingness to marry her to uphold the "code" that was important. He did not do so consciously: his was just the way of the true Westerner.

Grey was pleased when Dolly complimented *The Code of the West*, for he respected her judgments above all others. She wrote to him as she edited the novel: " . . . I like the story very much indeed. It is in a lighter vein than your others, yet does not be-little its title: 'The Code of the West.' Possibly it's a truer picture of real conditions than many you've done."[23] A few days after this letter from Dolly, Grey heard from the editor of *The Country Gentleman*, which serialized *The Code of the West* for thirty-thousand dollars. The editor told Grey: "At last you seem to have broken through the reserve of that New York bunch who scratch each other's back and who look upon the country West of the Hudson as largely waste territories from a literary standpoint."[24] For a man who had fought editors and critics for most of his adult life, Grey found these words most soothing.

The Western novels which made Zane Grey famous ranged in setting and subject from the deserts, mountains, and corrals to history, horseflesh, and humanity. Probably of all the types of Western novels Grey wrote, the writing of the straight cowboy story made him the most comfortable. Within the category of cowboys and Indians, Grey used a formula (proprietary thoughts about the land, practical joking, especially against a "greenhorn," and inevitability of clashes with Indians) that could very quickly be spotted by his readers. The only author of the time who e-qualed and surpassed Grey's output (but not sales) was Frederick Faust (Max Brand). These two filled the pages of pulp magazines, each writing so voluminously that even their most ardent fol-lowers had trouble keeping up with their productions.

As has been noted, Grey did not confine himself completely to stories of the West. He also attempted to write plays (usually in collaboration with someone); he produced a large amount of fic-tion about baseball, and he wrote several books and articles on fishing. He personified everything that a sporting-literary life could give to a man. Yet he suffered long, dreadful spells of de-pression as he went through his days of writing, traveling, and fishing. He talked at length sometimes in his diary about the brevity of life, and perhaps this preoccupation accounted for his occasional morbidity. Despite his personal feelings, however, he still managed to "grind out" the hundreds of thousands of words that delighted his readers.

CHAPTER 7

Short Works and Fishing Stories

In late October, 1922, Zane Grey told his wife that he planned to write ten short stories before Christmas,[1] This forecast was not unduly optimistic, for Grey's talents and his ability to write for sustained periods coincided with America's "Golden Age" of pulp magazines. It was a good time to write short stories. Most of Grey's short stories had, oddly enough, better characterization than his novels; for in his short pieces he intensified moods and personalities. As a result, some of Grey's best writing was in the form of the short story.

I Baseball and Western Short Stories

Grey's love for baseball inspired several short stories and articles. "The Winning Ball," published in *The Popular Magazine* in 1930,[2] was about a "rabbit" ball which, after the first bounce, was likely to take a huge leap away from the defensive player. When one of Grey's baseball stories, *The Young Pitcher*, was chosen by the United States government for use in Philippine schools, Dolly remarked to Grey that the selection " . . . is a landmark; one of the significant things that count."[3] *The Redheaded Outfield and Other Stories*, published in 1920, contained most of the significant Zane Grey baseball stories. Many, if not most, were reminiscences from Grey's early life when he himself played baseball. Though the main purpose of the stories was entertainment, there were enough baseball-playing factory workers leaving their jobs for the freedom of the diamond to allow Grey, perhaps inadvertently, to get in some social comment.

However, most of Grey's short stories, like his novels, dealt with the West. Thematic materials for his shorter works were essentially the same as in the novels: the life of a Texas lawman was described in "The Ranger"; the reform of wayward ways was delineated in "Canyon Walls"; brotherly love and sacrifice were featured in "Avalanche" and Monty Price's Nightingale"; repentance was the moving force of "The Secret of Quaking Asp Cabin"; and consolation was a large attribute in "Amber's Mirage." To a considerable extent, Grey's short stories were variants, therefore, of larger works for which he was already known. [4]

Grey discussed at length in some of his novels the Texas Rangers, so "The Ranger," a 1929 feature of *Ladies' Home Journal*, came as no surprise to his readers. Vaughn Medill of this story may have been the prototype of Texas Rangers, and he may have fully accepted the time-honored dictum "run the man down", but, when love and private enterprise offered the opportunity, he settled down to a peaceful life of farming and ranching. Throughout his writings, Grey praised private ownership of property and true love. Though the Rangers were highly dedicated, professional men, they still recognized that it is possible for men to change from their bad ways and become positive social forces. Such an event occurred not only in Grey's novel *Shadow on the Trail* but also in his short story "Canyon Walls." In this story, Monty Bellew enjoyed a happy married life for two years until the law caught up with him; but seeing what Monty had become rather than what he had been, caused the sheriff to leave him alone. Grey hinted that Monty's punishment for his past crimes was the constant dread of suddenly being deprived of his beloved wife and family—this fear was a greater penalty than anything the law could mete out to him.

Whereas Monty Bellew exemplified a man's efforts to live down his past, Monty Price, a featured cowboy in *The Light of Western Stars*, was the central figure in "Monty Price's Nightingale" who epitomized self-sacrifice. As a young cowboy, Monty Price was troublesome to his associates and was always cursed "in hearty cowboy fashion." When a forest fire broke out, Monty was faced with the responsibility of saving a small child, Del Muncie, from the flames. In carrying out his deed of heroism, Monty was horribly mangled; and he became a lonely man because of his disfigurement, who always listened to the plaintive song of the nightingale as it whistled away the nighttime hours. The song, somehow, gave outlet to the "passionate and irrepressible strain in his blood" that soothed him when he thought of his accursed physical appearance. The song, too, seemed to act as a joiner between two creatures of nature who had reached the heights of nobility. [5]

Grey used the idea of sacrifice in another short story, "Ava-

lanche," first published in 1928 by *The Country Gentleman*. The
setting was the Tonto Country where every emotion seemed to
be magnified over those of ordinary mortals. A man, Jake Dun-
ton, and his stepbrother Verde, fought for the affections of Kitty
Mains; and in time the two brothers became bitter enemies.
When Jake trailed Verde into Black Gulch Canyon, intent upon
killing him, an avalanche occurred, which caused survival to be
uppermost in Jake's mind. When Jake escaped the onslaught and
Verde was seriously injured, to save Verde became Jake's consuming passion. Jake had to amputate Verde's leg to combat gan-
grene, and then had to nurse the injured man for weeks before
leaving the area where the avalanche had happened. During the
period, the question of which one would win Kitty Mains was
thought of but rarely mentioned. When the two returned to civilization, they discovered that Kitty had been married for several
weeks. Sacrifice first and irony second were the major themes of
"Avalanche." This story was a popular one; and, apparently, it
was one of Grey's favorites as he frequently identified himself in
his manuscripts as the author of "Avalanche" and other stories.

Sacrifice can often be related in its effects to repentance. Grey
clarified this point in one of his best short stories, "The Secret
of Quaking Asp Cabin," printed in 1954 in *American Weekly*. The
first-person narrator of the story got lost from his camping group
in the Mogollons, and he wandered around until he came upon
a cabin in the midst of some asp trees. In the cabin was the im-
print of a bloody hand on the fireplace, and there were several
bullet holes scattered around the walls. The narrator marked the
place; and, when he had found his way back to camp, he tried to
get someone to tell him the story of the cabin.

Finally, a half-breed Apache told him that the first occupants of
the cabin had been Richard Starke; his wife, Blue; and his younger brother, Len. One day Richard saw Blue and Len making love
to each other; the two, who knew Richard had seen them, kept ex-
pecting him to do something, but he did not. When Richard was
shot, presumably by Len, his right arm and shoulder were blown
away, as well as the top of his lung; but, through sheer willpower
and hate, he survived the ordeal. Len left as soon as it was apparent that Richard would survive; but Blue stayed at the cabin,
to wait upon Richard for the rest of her days in atonement for her
wicked deed. The two did not speak to each other for ten years,
becoming, as it were, studies in grotesqueness. Finally, Richard
forgave his brother, and, when he had done so, he started to die,
since only his hatred had kept him going. One day he sat down in

his easy chair and spoke to Blue for the first time in a decade to
tell her that he forgave her and that he had invited Len to return.
As the hoof-beats of Len's horse were heard in the distance, Richard died. Such was the secret, the narrator discovered, of Quaking Asp Cabin.

The cabin was mentioned in other Grey works. For example,
some members of the notorious Hash Knife outfit used it as a
hideout on occasions. Its chief symbol, however, did not emanate
from outlawry but from betrayal, contrition, sacrifice, and forgiveness. Though the story was set in the Western regions, its
events and themes were universal in nature. Grey's story proved
that forgiveness for injuries sustained, both physical and mental,
was the most ennobling of all man's acts.

II   Grey As a Playwright

Mankind's ability to forgive was pursued by Grey in "Amber's
Mirage," which was both a play and a short story. The tale was an
allegorical explanation of the conflicts that arise from the love of
both gold and women. Though the play, co-authored by Grey
and Millicent Smith[6] was called *Amber's Mirage*, the leading
character was Ruby Low. Her husband, Luke, was a tall, comely
person, who found that even after marrying Ruby and fathering
her daughter, he still had to compete with Al Shade (her former
lover, who was away searching for gold) and Joe Raston (the villain, who loaned money to Ruby's mother in return for her promise that he would ultimately have her daughter). Amber, the prospector, was old, gray, blind, long, lean, with a desert-lined face;
and his mirage was "a city of amber an' gold risin' out of a lake
where the water was gentle an' blue, an' shed the sunlight with
a blindin' radiance." For all of its splendor, however, Amber's
mirage was a "lonely empty city . . . like a city built for people
who forgot or lost their way." Thus, the fanatical love that a man
could have for gold, and what seeking it could do to his soul was
explained.

The play grew in complication as the three men—Luke, Al
Shade, Joe Raston—competed for Ruby Low. Because Al Shade
returned with a load of gold and because Raston was already
wealthy, it appeared that Ruby would abandon Luke because
she loved money. The climax came when Ruby discovered that
her and Luke's baby was missing. The key to the entire story was
revealed when she looked at Luke and lamented the loss of "our
baby." It turned out that shrewd old Amber had "borrowed" the

little girl for a time, knowing full well what effect his "kidnapping" would have on Ruby's and Luke's relations with each other. The play ended with the baby's return and with Al Shade's decision to leave the area.

Of the plays that Grey collaborated on, *Amber's Mirage* was probably the best; for it was a faster moving, more complex effort than the other playwriting attempts of Grey. There is no evidence, however, that this play or any other play which Grey wrote or collaborated with was ever performed. A month after *Amber's Mirage* was copyrighted (April, 1929) as a play, it appeared as a short story in *Ladies' Home Journal*; and in that form the story received most of its attention. Even the most zealous supporters of Zane Grey were not too impressed with his "career" as a playwright.

Grey also tried to succeed as a dramatist with a 1930 play, *Port of Call*, again co-authored by Millicent Smith.[7] Grey, a frequent visitor to the South Seas, took long fishing trips to New Zealand and Australia; and one of his favorite places was Tahiti. In *Port of Call*, which was similar to *The Reef Girl*, (a novel which Grey wrote about Tahiti and the South Pacific, but one which was never published), Grey showed that the natives were debased by the white man's presence. Grey was impressed with the noble stature of the South Sea Islanders, and almost without exception every character in the play who spoke ill of them was a scoundrel. The story's main character was Guy Rotherick who intended to stop off at Papeete and live with his brother Harvey, a resident of the Islands for several years. Aboard the *S.S. Tahiti*, Guy met and fell in love with a half-caste Tahitian, Frannie Marlowe.

When Harvey met Guy, he adamantly pled that Guy leave; for Harvey, who had become degenerate while in the Islands, rationalized his own condition by saying that he wanted to spare Guy these travails. A trinity of evil forces, said Harvey, worked on white men in the Islands: the tropical sun stopped healthy activities and produced languor, indulgence in native women, and addictions to liquor. To "save" Guy, Harvey convinced Frannie that she should give up her amorous attachment to Guy. Thus, Harvey and Frannie staged a big courting session for Guy in which they deliberately planned that he discover them, and hoped he would be infuriated enough to depart. Harvey's vahine (woman), Turea, could not bear the monstrous sham that Harvey performed, so she told the whole sordid story to Guy. In the final scene, which showed Guy and Frannie sailing away on the *S.S. Tahiti*, they attracted some attention, and a passenger, Mr. Ovington, said to his wife: "These Island natives are a primitive people, not very far removed from the savage. It stands to reason that white inheritance can't combat that in a generation. They're all alike. They're children. That's why they are dangerous for a white man."

The most significant thing in *Port of Call* was Grey's making it clear to the reader that Ovington's statement was inane. The play, on the whole, was an attack against racism, for Grey brought into sharp focus the differences between the "advanced" white culture and the "primitive" natives, and showed that in most instances, the natives were the happier of the two. Grey, an admirer of Herman Melville, believed with the author of *Omoo* and *Typee*, that the white man in the Islands caused a decline in native well-being. Therefore, Grey opposed, as had Melville, the business of white traders, and the work of Christian missionaries for their appearance marked the beginning of native degradation. Other than emphasizing these points, *Port of Call* was weak in sustaining the reader's interest. The large amounts of dialogue and the little action caused the play to progress slowly. The problem (that of Harvey "saving" his brother, Guy) was not dramatic or crucial enough to be convincing.

Yet Grey persisted in writing plays. Another drama, with Millicent Smith's collaboration, was titled *Three Tight Lines* and set in the late 1920's in New York and in the woods of upper Maine.[8] This "comedy in three acts" was bad, even for melodrama. It started with three wives who lamented their status as "fishing widows" and who were planning a surprise visit to their husbands' camp in Maine. The husbands forgot to tell their wives that the camp cook was a last-minute substitution, a young lady named Mary Ann; and, just before the wives appeared on the scene, another woman, Hyacinth Hemming, had shown up after falling in the lake. She borrowed some dry clothes from Mary Ann, so the first thing the wives saw when they entered the cabin was the forsaken attire that belonged to Hyacinth. After several pages of confrontations between the wives and husbands, it developed that Hyacinth belonged to a bootlegging ring in that part of the country and that Mary Ann was part of the special police force sent to capture her. Once this was accomplished, and the misunderstandings cleared up, peace and love were restored.

The great difference between *Three Tight Lines* and *Port of Call* was that the clichés and the superficiality in the former were not shown to be in poor taste as in the latter; for Grey did not "editorialize" in *Three Tight Lines* as he did in *Port of Call*. Both plays were poorly written, but at least there was *some* substance in *Port of Call*. *Three Tight Lines* had people in it whose views and practices would have been condemned in any number of Grey's Western novels: they were shallow, unthinking, for the most part idle people, who really did not contribute to the betterment of the world. Grey was intolerant of such people in most of his writings.

III   Fish Stories

Fortunately, Grey did not spend too much time with plays; and he did write a very large number of fishing stories. Approximately one hundred fishing articles, either by Grey or about him, appeared in leading sports journals like *Sports Afield*, *Field* & *Stream*, and *Outdoor America*; and many of these articles were later printed in collected form in one of the nine major fishing books that Grey authored: *Tales of Fishes* (1919), *Tales of Southern Rivers* (1924), *Tales of Fishing Virgin Seas* (1925), *Tales of the Angler's Eldorado* (1926), *Tales of Swordfish and Tuna* (1927), *Tales of Fresh Water Fishing* (1928), *Tales of Tahitian Waters* (1931), *An American Angler in Australia* (1937), and *Zane Grey's Adventures in Fishing* (1952), edited by Ed Zern.

Grey hunted some, but his first love was fishing. The quiet boyhood joys of fishing along the banks of the Muskingum and Licking Rivers turned into boisterous assaults on huge inhabitants of the sea. Ocean trips brought out the pensiveness in Grey; for as he recorded in his diary, "The sea, from which all life sprung, has been equally with the desert my teacher and my religion," He related further that he never saw the sea until late in his college career, but he knew at once that it "would fulfill vague dreams."[9] His favorite sea-sites in the United States were Seabright (New Jersey) on the Atlantic, Long Key (Florida) on the Gulf of Mexico, and Avalon (California) on the Pacific. He also fished the waters off Nova Scotia; and there in 1924, he bought a sailing ship, *Fisherman I*, previously named *Marshall Foch*.[10]

Grey's first fishing book appeared in 1919 and was titled *Tales of Fishes*. A collection of articles, many of which had already been published in *Field* & *Stream*, the book described events and places from the Florida coast to the Indian Ocean. Grey enjoyed excellent reviews of *Tales of Fishes*: *The Boston Transcript* called it a volume "filled with matter that will arouse and hold the true fisherman's mind enthralled."[11] The *New York Times* said of the book: "Somehow the true atmosphere of the sea and its mystery has been caught and held throughout, and for all who love and long for real 'salt' there is a great treat awaiting."[12] Theodore Brooke, always a friendly reviewer of Grey's books, predicted that *Tales of Fishes* would become a classic "which all good followers of Isaac Walton will treasure";[13] and Robert Hobart Davis, a leading sportsman himself and editor of *Munsey Magazine*, chided Grey for not remembering to let Davis write an introduction to the book as promised.[14]

In *Tales of Southern Rivers*, a 1924 collection of stories and articles by Grey, two of the tales related fishing experiences in the Gulf stream and on the rivers of the Everglades. The third tale, "Down an Unknown Jungle River," was an account of adventures on the Santa Rosa River in the jungles of Mexico that Grey experienced in 1911. On this trip Grey and two companions eluded tigers and wild hogs, and they stoically reconciled themselves to torment from giant ticks. Two short stories, "Tigre" and "The Rubber Hunter," were inspired by Grey's visit to the wilds of Mexico. *The Springfield* (Massachusetts) *Republican* lavished praise upon the book: "Grey is noted for his descriptive powers. All his books carry this quality. But in this new book, he excels in this faculty and his knowledge of the equatorial wilderness and waters is spread before his reader in a way that is a treat for the lovers of outdoor life."[15]

Grey's fishing books gave insights into his philosophy and attitudes perhaps better than any of his other writings; for the vastness and the loneliness of the open sea enthralled, troubled, and depressed him. Whenever he lamented the brevity of life, he he was usually on a fishing trip or was planning one. He expressed all of these moods in his 1925 fishing book, *Tales of Fishing Virgin Seas*. When Grey was off the Cocos Islands, he pondered the ferocity of sharks fighting over fish carcasses: "Such swift action, . . . such unparalleled instinct to kill and eat! But this was a tropic sea . . . where life is so intensely developed . . . . The beauty was there to see, but not the joy of life" (24-25). Grey worried because he had heard stories about sharks attacking and sinking boats. Despite his anxieties, Grey comforted himself with the belief: "Thought and intelligence have considerable power over the primitive in man. That is the hope of progress in this world" (31). The Cocos Islands made Grey know that "there are places too primitive for the good of man—too strangely calling to the past ages and their deep instincts."

From the Cocos, *Fisherman I* sailed toward Marchenas and the Perlas Islands. Marchenas reminded Grey of the long ridges of the Arizona desert, and he became contemplative as a result: "The lure of the sea is some strange magic that makes men love what they fear. The solitude of the desert is more intimate than that of the sea. Death on the shifting barren sands seems less insupportable to the imagination than death out on the boundless ocean, in the awful windy emptiness. Man's bones yearn for the dust" (95-96). Grey believed that the fisherman grew, in time, to "regard all with tranquility, with the simplicity of the Indian . . ." (121-11). Such a stage in one's life, Grey argued, was the attainment of wisdom.

Throughout these musings, which Grey carefully recorded in his diaries, he and his crew were busy catching and observing fish. Grey was enchanted to see for the first time a sperm whale. He was entranced, too, by the evidence of evolution that was about him. In his Western novels, he spoke of evolutionary schemes, and the ocean only confirmed these truths. He frequently mentioned in this book Charles Darwin's voyage on the *Beagle*, and the influence on him that Darwin's books had had. Grey exclaimed: "Always the ocean was yielding some more superlative quality of beauty. Always the beauty! It seemed such a mystery to me. But perhaps Nature required beauty as well as other attributes in its schemes of evolution" (143).

Grey's most frequent reaction to the sights about him on this trip was the constant competition among the creatures of the sea. It was "survival of the fittest," the test to which all living things were subjected whether on the ocean or on the desert. He concluded that man, though having to conform to "natural selection," was equipped with a higher order of mental faculties than other animals. This gave man supremacy, at least to the extent that nature allowed any permanent alteration of her system. The littleness of man in relation to nature was a thought that Grey often expressed, for man was but an atom whirling around in a vast universe that he neither created nor controlled. The sea's splendor, its overpowering might, and its mystery, reflected the eternal; man was the image of transiency. It was not the sea alone that produced such thoughts in Grey, but it had a great influence in doing so.

Grey sailed for the South Pacific, largely as a result of New Zealand's invitation to publicize its fishing waters; and he spent the last day of 1925 at sea aboard the British mail ship, *S. S. Makura*. He was in a serious mood as he wrote in his diary and later in *Tales of the Angler's Eldorado*, a 1926 publication: "What was the old year to the sea, or the new year soon to dawn with its

imagined promise, its bright face, its unquenchable hope?" (4).
Perhaps preoccupation of one sort or another caused Grey on that
New Year's eve to smash his thumb in a door, inflicting a long and
painful, though not permanent, injury; and although Grey was
often querulous, his accident made it worse:

> . . . I smashed my thumb in the door. It is a very painful injury.
> Today I could not hold a pencil. Besides I was not well from the
> hurry and worry of preparation . . . [of leaving] . . . Was quite sick
> all day, with headache, cold, and fever from sore thumb. In the
> afternoon my left eye became greatly inflamed, so that at length I
> could not see out of it. Finally it closed completely . . . . Developed
> a congestion in my breast and it grew worse until midnight when it
> began to grow easier . . . . We are now in equatorial regions . . . and
> the climate is singularly enervating. No doubt it would be bad
> enough if I was perfectly well, which I am not. I couldn't walk five
> lengths of the deck without wanting to rest.[16]

In addition to these troubles, Grey found it difficult to adjust to
the English custom of "meals six times a day" and to "dinner at
bedtime."[17]

Things improved considerably for Grey in mid-January when
the *Makura* paid calls to Tahiti and other South Pacific Islands.
Grey reacted with interest to the things he saw. Papeete, for
example, was the "eddying point for all the riffraff of the South
Seas." Tahitian women presented a new race to Grey: "They had
large melting melancholy eyes." But the tourists angered Grey;
he wondered why they came all the way to Tahiti just to eat and
drink. After leaving French-ruled Papeete, Grey went to Roratonga, which was under British control. Liquor was prohibited
at Roratonga; and Grey, an abstainer, credited the fact with producing an advanced culture.

Finally the *Makura* arrived in New Zealand, where the name
of "Maui" was bestowed upon Grey in honor of the Great Fisherman legend of the Maoris (144). In addition to this honor, Grey
was astonished at the friendliness proffered to him. He wrote to
Dolly that the government wanted to extend everything to him
free: "Yesterday I had the Prime Minister's car! You should have
seen the people look."[18] His prominence in New Zealand caused
his friend Davis to write to him: "Isn't it enough for you to be the
world's best seller without being the world's greatest angler? Truly the Lord has been good to you."[19] It was a new world for Grey
as he toured the farming enterprises and fished the waters of New
Zealand; and the fishing he did caused him to exclaim: "How

often fishing leads a man to find beauty otherwise never seen!" (173).

Grey's popularity, however, did not last; for he wrote several articles for newspapers criticizing the New Zealander's methods of fishing. He chided the fishermen for using a three-pronged hook, which he believed was elementary and cruel, and he also criticized other New Zealand fishing equipment, as when he told the fishermen that placing the reel over a rod would simplify their job. The controversy finally became so intense that Grey refused to write any more articles for newspapers. However, the argument with New Zealanders did not keep Grey from returning every year from 1926 to 1929 to fish its rivers and streams. He was still a "household" word in the area, and he became an authority on New Zealand sheep farming. He wrote an article on this subject in 1927 for *Country Gentleman*, titled "Sheep Raising in New Zealand."

The materials that Grey collected on his trips to New Zealand were sufficient for four books and scores of articles. In addition to *Tales of the Angler's Eldorado*, he wrote *Tales of Swordfish and Tuna* in 1927, *Tales of Tahitian Waters* in 1931, and *An American Angler in Australia* in 1937.[20] As a result of his fishing expeditions, Grey became one of the world's most renowned sportsmen. In 1929 he held eleven world fishing records; in 1936, six. He was the first man ever to use a rod and reel to land a one-thousand-pound fish.[21] A sailfish, *Isiophorus greyi*, was named after him.[22] He used the sea to gain knowledge of life and of its evolution.

Another collection of Grey's fishing stories was brought out in 1928, titled *Tales of Fresh Water Fishing*. Included in this volume was "A Day on the Delaware," the first article that Grey ever published. The major point of the article was his regret over losing a huge pike. Grey apparently never outlived disappointment at failing to catch a fish, as Dolly wrote to Davis in 1929: " . . . losing a fish assumes to him [Zane] the proportions of Greek tragedy!"[23] Other articles in this well-accepted book included "Crater Lake Trout" and "Trolling for Trout at Pelican Bay" (both published by *Country Gentlemen* in 1920), "The Fighting Qualities of the Black Bass," (*Field* & *Stream*, 1912) and "The Lord of Lackawaxen Creek," (*Outing*, 1909). The prolonged popularity of such articles assured Grey a position as an authority on fishing and conservation. Though no evidence exists that Grey had read the works of Henry David Thoreau, he was much like the New Englander in relating to the outdoors.

Despite his successes, Grey still suffered rounds of melancholy. To Dolly he wrote in March, 1927: "I can't stand the truth. Realism is death to me. I cannot stand life as it *is*!"[24] A month later he said, "I have been and still am pretty badly discouraged . . . . I'm all right in the day time, but when I awake in the night, as I do every night, it is simply hell. I don't know what's wrong unless the exhaustion of the day makes me morbid at night . . . . It seems such an endless time since I left home and such an eternity until I get back."[25]

IV Significance of Fishing to Grey

In *Tales of Fresh Water Fishing*, Grey named William Radcliffe, "An English author and Oxford man," as the person most influential on his fishing moods and methods. Radcliffe's *Fishing from the Earliest Times* was such a great book in Grey's opinion that he did not feel equal to reviewing it for American publication. Nonetheless, he said of the book (building at the same time a great case for the fisherman):

> It [the book] is a treasure-mine of truth about the oldest sport and one of the earliest trades known to men. Fishing has history little suspected by the mass of men who love to follow it. My father used to punish me for running off to fish when I should have mowed the lawn or swept out his office. He declared the only good fishermen who had ever lived were Christ's four fishermen disciples. My father was sure I would come to some bad end because I loved to fish. But he was wrong. All the fathers of youthful Isaak Waltons or angling Rip Van Winkles should read this wonderful book and learn how fortunate they are in having such inspired sons. For fishing has a dignity, a simplicity, a ruggedness and honesty little dreamed of in this materialistic world. Its history is profoundly revealing and tremendously interesting to the angler, whether he be naturalist or not. But every fisherman, unconsciously or otherwise, is something of a naturalist (152-53).

Grey concluded his praise of Radcliffe's book by asserting that it invested fishing with the "dignity of education, of culture, of an affinity with great minds of the past, with an important place in the history and progress of the world" (154).

Though Grey obtained some of his profoundest thoughts while fishing, the "universal boy" in him probably motivated his expeditions to a considerable extent. He had a keen sense of competition, and he was never really content with any of his accomplishments. Life to Grey, then, was movement from one high plane to another high plane in his "quest for the unattainable." When Grey sometimes abstained from fishing for months, he would hear that one of his records had been broken and off he would go to recapture his title. Sprotsman Ed Zern, who edited *Zane Grey's Adventures in Fishing,* said: "If he [Grey] had landed a ten ton serpent on 39-thread line he would almost certainly have fretted over reports of a twenty-ton sea serpent sighted off the coast of Madagascar. What's more, he might have gone and caught it."[26] Fortunately for his readers, Grey usually wrote down his thoughts in diaries before he reached the areas of the big fish. These reflections often became the basis for the next novel or short story about the American West.

Not only the oceans and seas thrilled and invigorated Grey and inspired him to write; fresh water fishing delighted him as well. He frequently visited the Rogue River and the Umpqua River in Oregon. He stated once that "the happiest lot of any angler would be to live somewhere along the banks of the Rogue River, most beautiful stream of Oregon."[27] He bought a cabin at Winkle Bar on the Rogue, and spent many quiet, happy hours of contemplation there.

Early in his career as a fisherman, Grey felt twinges of conscience about hurting his victim. In 1918, he rationalized the sport; and at the same time he offered an insight into his reasons for writing: "As a man, and a writer who is forever learning, fishing is . . . tempered by an understanding of the nature of primitive man, hidden in all of us, and by a keen reluctance to deal pain to any creature. The sea and the river and the mountain have almost taught me not to kill except for the urgent needs of life . . . . When I read a naturalist or a biologist, I am always ashamed of what I have called a sport. Yet one of the truths of evolution is that not to practice strife, not to use violence, not to fish or hunt, that is to say, not to fight, is to retrograde as a natural man."[28] Grey came to believe that catching fish was only incidental to the true purposes of his expeditions. To study the "infinite" sea, and to exult over a "shaded and murmuring stream" was the real objective; and it provided him a sort of transcendental experience of unity with nature.

The sea and fresh water did not always put Grey into a philosophical frame of mind, for as indicated in his *Field & Stream* article, "Avalon, the Beautiful" (1918), he was angered during World War I by Austrian and Japanese fishing activities around Catalina Island off California. Fishing interests from these two countries netted huge amounts of white sea bass which were used for fertilizer. Moreover, the Austrians gathered kelp, from which potash, useful for war purposes, was made. Grey believed that the United States government should prohibit fishermen from these two countries, especially since the United States was at war against Austria at the time.[29]

Grey showed with this article ("Avalon, the Beautiful"), as well as others, that he did not fear controversy. He did not "glory" in it, but he joined the issue on things that really mattered to him. In the mid 1930's when he wrote some articles in *Sports Afield* favoring lever-action rifles,[30] he was criticized by supporters of bolt-action rifles, one critic saying that Grey was a "kitchen mechanic" author who should stick to his fishing.[31] Grey closed his side of the argument by asserting that the real culprit attacking lever-action rifles was the United States Army which believed that, if hunting was going on, it might as well be done with rifles similar to those used in the military. This instance was not the first one in which Grey blamed the government for supporting a practice he did not approve.

As a novelist, sportsman, and world traveler, Grey attained international fame. He was the spokesman for the great American West and for the world's fishermen. When he had obtained enough wealth through his writings to do generally as he pleased, his stature grew with every word he wrote. He may not have been the most eloquent or the most accomplished author in the world, but he was highly competent. Americans have long put much value in pragmatic, rather than theoretical things; and perhaps this pragmatism, built into America since colonial times, turned Grey into a phenomenally successful author and sportsman. He was direct in his descriptions and accounts, and was able to give his readers a keen sense of participation. He wrote to such an extent and to such a depth about American institutions that he almost became one himself. His readership of several millions proved him to be a literary force and a sports authority whose influence is still quite significant.

CHAPTER *8*

Zane Grey: Writer

Zane Grey's successful career as a writer was a case of the times and the man meeting each other at the most opportune moment, for Grey visited and roamed the West at probably the best of all possible periods. The West was still wild—with plenty of animal and climatic difficulties—but the real hardships confronted by the first settlers had passed. Yet, Grey's relationship with the West came before the tourism that altered so much of the area's natural beauty. Grey saw the wild West when pioneer conditions no longer prevailed, but before the modern era had begun; and this fact may have been instrumental in his constant romanticizing of the American West.

He brought with him to the West a deep respect for natural beauty. He loved naturalness so much that he would not allow leaves to be raked from the garden at his home in Altadena, California.[1] His regard for the natural state of things was ingrained into him early in life. His first twenty years were spent in essentially rural and small-town settings, and these influences worked steadily on him. Grey's love of nature came first in his order of priorities, then love of literature, and third, love of the West. These three attributes worked in combination to produce Grey's literary career.

Grey possessed a lively curiosity and an independent mind, both qualities apparent even in his youth when he wrote "Jim of the Cave" and when he disputed points of protocol with his teachers. These two characteristics, plus a desire to write, were vital to a literary career. Grey's writing talents were latent, and it took several years of vigorous effort to make him a success. The greatest influence on Grey was Dolly, but he also read technical books on writing and developed his own "rules for literary work."[2] These guidelines were so important to Grey that they deserve extensive quotation.

1 Grey's Literary Rules

The first part of his literary rules dealt with reading. A book should be read creatively, "that is, slowly, repeatedly, carefully, resolving allusions, following suggestions, . . . until thoroughly imbued with the power and thought of the writer."[3] Every day, he believed, one should read selections of Shakespeare, Tennyson, Hugo, Tolstoi, Stevenson, James, and Wordsworth. Grey indicated the influences of certain authors when he wrote: "Hawthorne awakens in me a cold purity of sensation, a mystic soul-perception of beauty, of shadow, of spiritual life. How solitary and sweet must have been his thoughts! He must have been a watcher with a sympathetic heart, yet aloof and self sufficient. I can see compassion in his dark eye as he gazes upon the lives of people. Dearest souled of men, he searched for and found the fountain of wisdom. From him I learn of moral evil and moral good. Arnold's poetry lights the white flame in my heart . . . . His sadness, his melancholy, his dreams, are mine."[4] Wordsworth was valuable to Grey also; nice weather one day after a bad spell caused him to exclaim that he had just received a "Wordsworth uplift."[5]

The second part of Grey's literary rules urged him always to keep eyes and ears open for new ideas: "Look at things so keenly as to find unknown characteristics, unsuspected points of view, secret depths, the life & soul of natural facts."[6] A writer must constantly study nature, men, and women, said Grey, so that "every situation would yield significance for thought." This procedure enabled an author to develop "self-culture" in which he would always "live among beautiful thoughts."[7]

After these generalizations concerning his literary objectives, Grey turned his attention to particulars—to detailed and intricate methods of composition. On writing's basic unit, the sentence, he instructed himself (probably with the help of Clayton Hamilton and J. H. Gardiner):

Think what the sentence is to exist for—what is its central thought. Do not crowd in irrelevant thoughts. Do not change subject if it can be helped. Be watchful of pronouns. Keep participles within the body of sentence, and watch their subjects . . . adverbial adjuncts must adhere closely to the words they are intended to modify. Do not hang a relative clause upon another relative clause. Cut out intensive expression and superlatives that are unnecessary. beware of "but," "it," and "there." Cut them out when possible. The skill with which a writer deals with the small connecting words, particles, and pronouns is the best evidence of the extent to which he has attained a mastery of the art of composition. Adapt sound to sense: as the hum of the bee. The hiss of the serpent. The whistling of the wind. Work for clearness, sequence, climax. Do away with conjunctions, if possible, except when the meaning changes. Do not suppress subject. Do not use second person. Do not use italics except ,in dialogue. A proper variety requires that periodic sentences should be used: have a care of these. Make the meaning plain, and give it all the force possible. This last important point in any given sentence is secured by attending chiefly to the position of the principal subject and the principal predicate, and by placing these words so that in reading they are naturally and easily emphatic. Be careful to have infinite variety of sentences; intersperse periodic sentences occasionally with those that are loose. Avoid sameness of stress and emphasis. Long and short sentences help variety. Be familiar with equivalents of the relatives. Think or write sentence over several ways before finally committing it. Brevity helps action and makes strength and force.[8]

Grey violated these rules a number of times as he wrote his novels, short stories, and articles; but such entries in his diaries proved that, contrary to what some critics said, he did have a concern for the technical aspects of writing.

Rules for paragraphing also were important to Grey: "Write topic sentence at beginning, and endeavor to have succeeding sentence amplify and grow out of preceding. Parallel construction aids delicacy of effect . . . . The subject should be clearly determined in the writer's mind, if not stated in the paragraph." Grey said "eternal vigilance is the price of a good style." A writer should learn to phrase thoughts in his mind without putting them on paper and to become a ruthless self-critic. Also, fledgling writers, as well as fully accomplished ones, should study the masterpieces of literature because this was the best way to improve stylistic sensitivity.

Most critics agreed that Grey's strongest talent was in the power of description. Grey wrote in his diary that description should appeal to memory and reason: "A cunning writer will avail himself of images likely to be stored in the minds of his readers; with appeal to their emotions, to the general experiences of mankind." He believed, too, that, in viewing a scene, the mind should dwell on the impression first, allowing the observer to select the central idea. After the impression of the scene was formed, the writer could go ahead with the description, which should evolve from the simple to the complex. Original descriptions, Grey believed, came from "traits, epithets, and thought which people have used before" but which have been "fused anew" in the mind of the writer and used as a "new force."

Grey asserted that a writer had a responsibility to say what he thought was wrong with society. He did so in a number of novels, *The Day of the Beast* and *The Vanishing American* being particularly significant in this respect. As early as his 1905 diary entries, Grey had formed these conclusions: "The author must so thoroughly understand human nature that he will know exactly what and how great a motive is necessary for a certain act of a certain person . . . . The great gift of a writer is sincerity. A writer must have strong and noble convictions about life."[9] In communication with Murphy, Grey expostulated on the importance of being natural: "As there is no possibility of me ever becoming sophisticated, I may as well be natural . . . . Isn't to be natural a great strength in writing? [Herbert] Spencer says the natural style, that in which he—the writer, writes as he thinks and feels, ought to be the aim of every literary aspirant."[10]

II Grey, a "Loner" in Literature

Zane Grey did have "strong and noble" convictions about life, and he attempted to incorporate them into his novels. His thoughts on strength and nobility, however, differed sharply from those held by most other writers of the day, because he felt that a novelist should be something of a crusader, but at the same time he should delineate positive as well as negative forces at work in society. It was his philosophy and his difference from others that caused Grey to turn his back on most contemporary literature and to become a "loner," that person of the West that he described in so many of his books.

Grey also objected to the coterie of naturalist writers who gained some prominence in the first part of the century. He believed that some of their work was worthwhile, but their pose as authorities on wild life caused Grey some consternation. As he said in a letter to Murphy: "Stewart White I never met. I think his work, what I have read, good and reliable, but . . . [Ernest] Seton and [Jack] London are pure fakes, as far as animals go. What they write is as the President [presumably of the United States—probably Theodore Roosevelt] said—a closet product."[11]

In part, his unconventional relationship to current literature caused Grey to range from spells of moroseness to self-righteous defiance. A 1917 diary entry, for example, showed that he was

at least conscious of his problem: "A hyena lying in ambush—
that is my black spell!—I conquered one mood only to fall prey
to the next. And there have been days of hell. Hopeless, black,
morbid, sickening, exaggerated, mental disorder! I know my
peril—that I must rise out of it, very soon for good and all, or
surrender forever. It took a day—a whole endless horrible day
of crouching in a chair, hating self and all, the sunshine, the
sound of laughter, and then I wandered about like a lost soul, or
a man who was conscious of imminent death. And I ached all
over, my eyes blurred, my head throbbed, and there was pain
in my heart. Today I began to mend and now there is hope."[12]

His tendencies toward depression did not really endanger
his literary career; on the contrary, they probably assured it.
Such entries reflected Zane Grey, the overly sensitive man,
rather than Zane Grey, the really depressed man. Grey worried
about things: slow royalty checks, World War I, the well-being
of his family, things costing more than he anticipated, critics,
and, to a very great measure, success itself. He seemed to feel
a bit frightened about being a "winner" in the literary field, and
it is doubtful that he would ever have made such over-dramatized
inclusions in his diary if he had not been an author to begin with.
Dolly noted his tendency toward self-pity when she upbraided
him for condemning everything and everybody for the unsettled conditions of the time and for his turgid frame of mind.[13] To
a degree, statements in letters and diaries that reflected moods
of dejection were simply his ways of reconciling himself with the
world in which he lived; they were not symptoms of a deep-
rooted or permanent difficulty.

World War I troubled Grey, for the war was a bad time, he
said, for a thinking man, and fatal for an idealist.[14] Apparently,
he believed with eminent historian Carl Becker that the preceding century of historical research was worthless because it
did not prevent World War I.[15] Like Becker, Grey felt that history should be primarily a social force. His feelings of helpless-
ness in the midst of historic events was most intense. He said,
"I feel like an atom whirling in a universe of winds."[16] The war
caused him to quote three of his favorite authors: "Tennyson
wrote 'Through all the ages an increasing purpose runs.' Perhaps!
And maybe civilization is progressing. Stevenson wrote: 'surely
not all in vain!' . . . I am low-spirited these days. Wordsworth
wrote: 'The world is too much with us,' and 'where is the glory
and the dream?' . . . of yesterday, he meant, the flower and the
beauty and the life that has gone! Something dark and gloomy

borders my spirit. I must work and move about, and cease brooding."[17]

Grey's anti-Germanism during the war and his obvious sympathy for the American soldier made his books the most popular
ones with the masses and the "dough-boys." As an executive at
Harper's explained this popularity," . . . Your books were the
first choice of the soldiers and . . . the spirit that was in them
rather than the adventure was what made them strong in their
belief that Zane Grey is the great American writer of his day."[18]
Grey was delighted, also, to be told that, if he continued to live
in the open, "loving nature, loneliness, etc., . . . I could die the
greatest writer of America."[19] John Wannamaker, who once told
Grey, "never lay down your pen," believed that President Harding should send Grey to Russia to interpret America.[20] Grey's
popularity was capped when Macy's Department Store in New
York started selling a new colored paint, "zane gray." Harper's
was so impressed with the idea that Grey's books were covered
with the dustjackets of this "color."

After the war, Grey lamented the apparent indifference of the
government toward veterans. Though Grey generally supported
Republicans, he disagreed with the vetoes of veteran pension
bills by President Harding and President Coolidge. He wrote
several novels that dealt with the plight of World War I veterans,
The Call of the Canyon and *The Shepherd of Guadaloupe* being
perhaps the most prominent. Other authors, of course, attacked
this problem, but their way of doing so apparently did not please
Grey. He objected to the new psychological trends of the day,
and to increasing emphasis on sex in such books.

How Grey felt about certain types of modern literature was
shown by an exchange of letters between Dolly and R. H. Davis.
Grey read John O'Hara's *Appointment at Samarra*, and on its
back cover were lavish praises of it by reviewers, including Doro-
thy Canfield and Alexander Woolcott. Dolly said: "To me these
laudings smelled of people who were afraid of being Victorian or
not modern if they didn't swallow a particularly nauseous dose
of medicine with a broad smile. The book is clever, it is true to
certain phases of modern existence, it more or less comes within
the experience which most of us are acquainted with, but I ask
you, aren't certain things better left to the imagination? Should
Mr. O'Hara be called 'courageous' for writing it? I somehow see
him laughing at the adjective."[21]

Dolly admitted that she looked at O'Hara's book through her
bias for her husband: "The man [Zane] has always lived in a land

of make-believe, and has clothed all his own affairs in the shining garments of romance, and it is as if these were rent and torn and smirched."[22] In agreeing with Dolly about Zane's status in literature, Davis replied: ". . . The trend in literature is along the O'Hara lines, a little dirtier, I imagine, and I trust better written . . . Zane is a naturalist. Zane is a disciple of the horse and buggy days . . . . I prefer Zane's reserve, while deploring his lack of familiarity with the world, the flesh and the devil. We ought to be glad he's that way."[23]

Grey constantly worried about his literary standing because of the popularity of the kind of fiction he did not write. To the mid-1920's, he fretted over reviewers who sometimes were not at all kind to him. Dolly helped with these difficulties by writing: "A lot of these second-rate reviewers and writers would give their immortal souls to do what you're doing. What if you're not a high-brow? If you were, thousands & thousands whom you are delighting & helping would never read you."[24] Despite such assurances, Grey continued his anxieties: "I am worried about my stories and the modern trend. Such books that are published now! I am afraid that pretty soon no one at all will read me. Do you ever feel that way?"[25] Less than a month before his death, however, Grey was autographing his books in a department store at the rate of five per minute, finally having to stop because of exhaustion.[26] Clearly, therefore, Grey never really ran the risk of the catastrophe that he feared so much, that of becoming an outdated author.

III Grey's Contemporaries

Frederick Faust (Max Brand) was a contemporary of Grey's, and the two were easily the most authoritative novelists on the West. Brand produced a more "action type" story than Grey, and he was not too concerned with descriptions and the expressions of moods. When Grey died in 1939, he had sixty published books to his credit. Through 1944, the year of Faust's death, one hundred twenty-eight books had appeared under his various pseudonyms. Yet Grey occupied the best-selling lists for nine years; Faust never once. The great difference between the two authors, according to one opinion, was that Grey wrote about the West as he imagined it; Faust wrote about the West as he dreamed it. He felt that if he could not dream a story, he could not write it.[27]

Grey's affinity for history helped also to produce the differences between the two men. In 1893, historian Frederick Jackson Turner delivered his famous speech on the importance of the frontier to American history. He pointed out that, as of 1890, census figures indicated that the Western frontier was no longer open. Turner's thesis dealt with the idea that more democracy existed in the West than in the East; that if one wished to learn the origin of American democratic institutions, he would have to study the West. Both Grey and Faust wrote when the Turner thesis was popular among historians and was known just enough by the middle classes to generate some interest. Grey's work had a more historical ring to it than Faust's, and this quality, in conjunction with ideas already made prominent by Turner, made Grey the most significant Western novelist of the time. Moreover, Grey always visited the places he wrote about, and his output was almost entirely Western. Faust, on the other hand, lived in Italy for several years while writing his books; and his interests ranged beyond the Western type story.[28]

Another writer, contemporary to Grey, whose creation became more famous than he himself, was Edgar Rice Burroughs, author of the "Tarzan" series. Burroughs and Grey, along with Faust, caused something of a revolution in the movie industry,[29] which tried to film everything they created. The stories were set on different continents, but essentially the same types of emotions and incidents prevailed. Burroughs liked to end his books on a note that necessitated a sequel. Grey did this too, but not to the same extent.[30] Despite the care which both men exercised in their work, their books were banned in at least one elementary school in California, Grey's for obscenities, and Burroughs' for portraying Tarzan and Jane in love with each other without benefit of marriage. Such an interdiction ranked high as one of the country's silliest escapades in the twentieth century.

Still another contemporary of Grey's who wrote for the masses was James Oliver Curwood. What Grey was to the Western, Curwood was, in large part, to the "Northern." Like Grey, he lived among the people he described in his pages. Like Grey, also, Curwood realized one day that his hunting expeditions were actually helping to destroy the nature he loved, so he put away his rifles and guns to become, with Grey, one of America's most prominent conservationists. Curwood died before Grey (1927), but the two careers were concurrent enough for Grey and Curwood to be hailed as great authors.[31]

The Grey-Faust-Burroughs-Curwood "combine" was an echelon below the Hemingway-Fitzgerald-Anderson-Lewis productions in the view of most critics. Grey and the authors like him were not debunkers: they did not deal solely with what had gone wrong in America, though they emphasized that point on a number of occasions. They were not members of a "lost generation"; instead, they wanted to point out the essentially positive aspects of the country and to show that its past indicated a brighter future than many of the most prominent contemporary writers were willing to accede. Too, they were not content merely to show the weaknesses in the American system; they gave many possible solutions as well. In the manner of the muckrakers whose most powerful influences came between 1900 and 1910, Grey and his followers managed to bring attention to many problems of high priority.

Grey's total output was nothing short of phenomenal, especially since he wrote entirely in long-hand and since he sometimes went for days without composing anything. The volume was accounted for by sustained, feverish work periods when he did get started. As a diary entry indicated, Grey had troubles with writing: "There is always an extreme difficulty in the taking up again the habit of writing. I wonder if this is because a relapse from literary work forms another habit. At any rate I am tortured before I can begin to write. This morning I had no desire to write, no call, no inspiration, no confidence, no joy. I had to force myself. But when I mastered the vacillation and dread, and had done a day's work—what a change of feelings. I had a rush of sweet sensations."[32] He had enough "sweet sensations" in his exceedingly busy life to write eighty-five books (twenty-five of which were published after his death), scores of articles, several diaries, and an average of five letters—long, involved ones—a day.

His work could, at times, produce confidence in him: "I believe absolutely in myself, my singular place, my gifts, my force . . . My zeal to work, my destiny . . . all I need is time—years to fulfill work. But dreaming so much I let the years slip by. Yet in 10 years I have written 19 books, none of which are equal to my ability. I have never spent myself. I am capable of great work."[33] Such exultant promises were tempered, however, by pessimism: "It is a terrible time. The seething revolution of the age affects me adversely, and forces me to think there is no use to write on. But I am compelled to."[34] The act of writing, then, caused Grey's moods to fluctuate between optimistic outlooks and gloomy reflections.

Often his state of mind, at least to the mid-1920's, depended upon how the critics viewed him at any given moment. They frequently tended either to ignore his work altogether or brutally to assault it. Both approaches were intensely unsettling to Grey. When he was attacked by reviewers, he usually aired his feelings in private to Dolly and in his diaries. A review of one of his novels (which he did not name) "was so bitter, so hateful, so amazingly unjust and false that it made me ill."[35] Several reviewers took the point of view that Grey's books were not true to life, and that the characters he created were not realistic. Grey's popularity remained, therefore, a mystery to them when a check with the middle- and lower-middle classes of the rural and small-town areas of the United States would have provided their answer. The reviewers reached the limit when they began hinting and then broadly asserting that the huge fish Grey caught were largely fiction. Grey was so angered that he wrote that such tactics "will eventually drive me to defend my reputation."[36]

IV Defense Against the Critics

He did defend his reputation in a lengthy treatise, written in the mid-1920's, but never published: "My Answer to the Critics." He had taken the critics too seriously, he said, in the first part of his career and had thus always been too humble toward them. In his quest to write permanent literature, he had wanted a "great audience. I chose to win that through romance, adventure, and love of the wild and beautiful in Nature. The West appealed tremendously to my imagination. I recognized it as one of the greatest fields for an American novelist . . . . I hoped and I prayed that the critics would judge me not from the result but from the nature of my effort."[37]

He noted his familiarity with the literary works of Wordsworth, Tennyson, Arnold, Ruskin, Stevenson, Jeffries, Hudson, Defoe, and Bunyan and with the Bible. He was not "anti-intellectual," as some critics said, because he was a graduate of a school that rivaled Harvard—the University of Pennsylvania, a school that "not so long ago . . . honored me with a degree of letters." Grey was born and raised in Ohio, as was Sherwood Anderson, the man to whom most contemporary Realistic critics gave first place in the ranks of American novelists. Grey said he was familiar with the type of people Anderson talked about, and he knew Anderson was wrong: "Mr. Anderson may be a very great writer. But if so, why did he not use his gifts toward the betterment of the world?

Why not write of the struggle of men and women toward the light? He is a destroyer, not a builder."

On the charge that he created unbelievable characters, Grey said that he had known a hundred cowboys like Venters (*Riders of the Purple Sage*), and dozens of Western girls who were as "sweet and innocent, and ignorant of life" as Bess Erne (*Riders of the Purple Sage*), Lucy Bostil (*Wildfire*) and Fay Larkin (*The Rainbow Trail*). Grey thought it singular that only the Eastern newspapers and periodicals printed adverse criticisms of his work, for "Seldom does a critic West of the Mississippi accuse me of falsifying character. Never of action or setting. Western people know I am absolutely true to the setting of my romances."

Grey reached the height of his impassioned plea for fairness from the critics when he wrote: "Who reads my books? Ask your janitor, your plumber, the salesgirl in the department store, the librarians, the firemen and the engineers, the carpenters, your lawyers, your doctors, the preachers who snatch a few hours for fiction out of their crowded lives, the school girls and boys, the teachers, the trained nurses, the farmers, the convicts in jail, the baseball players, the actors—John Barrymore, if you like— the motion-picture people, and the millions who support the screen. Ask anybody, ask New Englanders. I have an amazing public in Boston. Ask anybody but your brother critics. They do not know."[38]

After spending himself so emotionally on the question of the critics, Grey said he would never be bothered by them again; and he was not. He ignored the barbs, continued writing his books and stories at a fantastic rate, and stayed high in the ranks of popular writers. During his lifetime, *Riders of the Purple Sage*, *The Light of Western Stars*, and *Wildfire* were favorites of the public.[39]

V *Impact of Grey's Books*

Grey reached the height of his popularity in the United States between 1914 and 1928. That period was marked by war and then by social change in the 1920's. It was an affluent time when the average citizen was sports-minded, fun-loving, and movie-going. He was also "addicted" to his newspaper, especially the newly developing "Sunday sections." There was a growth in culture for the masses, a "democratization" of entertainment. Grey and his works fit very well into this picture. He could be used by the escapist for relief from the never-ending boredom of assembly lines; and, for those of the 1920's who wished to learn something about the generation of their fathers, Grey offered the opportunity. The bulk of Grey's audience, however, was the unsophisticated masses who still remembered enough of the rapidly passing rural scenes of America to wish they were back there. Grey enabled them to return vicariously to such settings, using the West for the purpose; and his reader was likely to identify quickly with the settings that Grey created. Those who revolted against the modern trends of industrialism and liberalized thinking turned to Grey. There was not just one single reason, therefore, for people to read Grey's books. The multiple uses of his work assured him a lasting place in American literature.

Grey's contribution to the Western novel in American literature was his greatest accomplishment. No other writer in this genre has yet approached his output and his sustained popularity. He wrote in a more descriptive and philosophical style than do most contemporary writers on the West. A present day western novelist, Tom Curry, explains it this way: the . . . "magnetism which draws and compels people to read his [Grey's] works . . . is elusive, and difficult to define; also it cannot be taught in any fashion. Technique may be, but the ability of a creative writer to hold his public is apparently inborn, some magic the author brews with the words he puts down, the fashion in which he delivers his thoughts, carrying his readers along in a grand sweep to the end."[40] Grey was a writer for the masses—those millions throughout the world who have long been fascinated with the American West, and the role it has played in American cultural history. To many minds, the West today still possesses the romantic qualities of a century ago, and this thought surely has helped Zane Grey's works to remain prominent.

In a less noticeable, but equally important, way, Grey's contributions to the conservation movement in the United States are highly significant. In dozens of articles he lamented wasteful practices—whether perpetrated by sportsmen or by business corporations. In numerous novels he railed against factions that were apparently bent upon scourging the land of its timber and other resources for economic gain, and against various governmental policies toward herds of wild animals. Despite all of this, Grey's view was a positive one; when he criticized his country, it was more out of love for it than repulsion.

His books that have remained the most prominent and popular through the years include *Riders of the Purple Sage, Wildfire,*

The U.P. Trail, Light of Western Stars, Heritage of the Desert, To The Last Man, Nevada, The Vanishing American, Western Union, and *The Maverick Queen.* Perhaps their popularity is due to their movie versions which are still shown periodically on television; perhaps, too, because they are faster moving than some of his other productions (thus fitting most quickly into changed reading habits which demand a lot of action), and have personalities within them (such as in *The Vanishing American*) that can be identified and sympathized with.

Grey should be judged on the quality of his total output and of his best books rather than on the weaknesses of some of his books. The picture that evolves of Grey reveals him to be a chronicler of events of the Old West, who had enough analytical power to give his work a historical aspect. His main strength was description; his main weakness was characterization. The picture of Grey shows, too, a concerned citizen disturbed over the abrupt changes occasioned by war. He became a social commentator, who never equaled people like Upton Sinclair in this respect, but who nevertheless had an impact upon certain individuals, not the least of whom were important conservationists. Finally, this picture of Grey shows him as a man of great sensitivity and ability, with an active, almost naïve, curiosity about the life around him. Possessed with an indefatigable energy, Grey believed in a rugged, outdoor life, feeling that a man's longevity would be increased as a result. (Grey was five feet eight inches tall, and kept his weight at around one hundred fifty pounds). He even went to the trouble of installing a fishing rod attached to heavy weights on the porch of his home at Altadena so he could stay in condition for for the next fishing expedition. Shortly after exercising with the rod, Grey suffered a fatal heart attack on the morning of October 23, 1939. He was 67 years old.

His death attracted world-wide attention, with so many tributes to him that a Harper's executive wrote to Dolly: ". . . I had no idea that some of the reviewers loved him and so many admired his work."[41] Dolly wrote to a friend that Grey's death was sudden and unexpected: "It seems to me that he is just away on one of those adventurous trips he loved so well—and perhaps his is."[42] Though the critics often scorned Grey for his characterizations, they almost universally agreed that he was a good storyteller, and that tales of adventure were his forte.

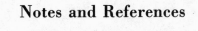

Notes and References

Notes and References

Chapter One

1. Charles McKnight, *Our Western Border* (Cincinnati, 1876), Grey's favorite character in this book was "Captain Jack of the Juniata." Even a cursory glance at the book shows its great impact on Grey in writing the Ohio River trilogy.
2. *The Living Past* is an unpublished autobiography which tells the story of his life through college days. All of the direct quotations in this chapter, not otherwise indicated, are from *The Living Past*. Grey Collection, Zane Grey, Inc.
3. Frank Gruber, author of the official biography of Grey, said that the patient was none other than Dolly, Grey's future wife.
4. Daniel Murphy to Grey, December 27, 1907. Grey Collection, University of Texas.
5. R. R. Brown to Charles Francis Press, February 1, 1904. Grey Collection, University of Texas.
6. Fannie Burns to L. M. Gray, January 20, 1904. Grey Collection, University of Texas.
7. C. M. L. Wiseman to Grey, February 1, 1904. Grey Collection, University of Texas.
8. Eugene H. Roseboom and Francis P. Weisenberger, *A History of Ohio* (Columbus, 1953), pp. 40-41 discusses this and other frontier events.
9. Eleanor Early, "He Made the West Famous," *True West*, XVI (April, 1969), 20. See also Norris Schneider, *Zane Grey, "The Man Whose Books Made the West Famous"* (Zanesville, Ohio, 1967), and *Zane Grey, The Man and his Work* (a compilation), (New York, 1928).
10. Zane Grey, *Diary*, October 1, 1905. Grey Collection, Zane Grey, Inc.

Chapter Two

1. For additional information on the "cattalo," see Lowell H. Harrison, "The Incredible Cattalo," *American History Illustrated*, II (January, 1968), 32-35. One of Jones's rivals in producing "cattalo" was Charles Goodnight, a rancher in the Texas Panhandle. Goodnight accused Jones of breeding the "cattalo" on paper, but not on the ground. Goodnight said of Jones: "Jones has been quite a hunter, and has been over a great deal of the Northwest.

.In that country they have great wind storms, known as 'chinook' winds. They are warm and harmless, but the Colonel seems to have got in one of these storms and imbibed [sic] immense quantities of hot air. It has been escaping from him ever since—mostly from the wrong end." J. Evetts Haley, *Charles Goodnight, Cowman and Plainsman* (Norman, Oklahoma. 1949), p. 453.

2. Robert Easton and Mackenzie Brown, *Lord of Beasts, The Life of Buffalo Jones* (London, 1964), pp. 146-47.

3. "My Own Life," cited in Grey, *Zane Grey, The Man and His Work* (New York, 1928), p. 4.

4. *Ibid.*, p. 5.

5. Grey to Daniel Murphy, undated, Markham Collection, Wagner College.

6. *History of Finney County Kansas* (Garden City, Kansas, 1950) I, 114.

7. "The Man Who Influenced Me Most," *American Magazine*, (August, 1929), 52-55; 130-36.

8. *Ibid.*, p. 53.

9. *Ibid.*, p. 54.

10. *Ibid.*, p. 136.

11. The prototype for August Naab was Jim Emett, the man who influenced Grey the most on Grey's Western trip. Emett's oldest son, who had no use for either Jones or Grey, was named Snap.

12. Silvermane actually existed. Grey, along with Jones and Jim Emett, tried several times to capture the animal. "The Man Who Influenced Me Most," p. 136, tells the difference between Jones and Emett in reference to wild animals. Jones mastered them through making them fear him; Emett, through making them love him. Grey preferred Emett's method to that of Jones.

13. Grey to Daniel Beard, June 6, 1910. Beard Collection, Library of Congress.

14. "My Own Life," p. 18.

15. "What the Desert Means to Me," *American Magazine*, 98 (November, 1927), 7.

16. *Diary*, January 19, 1919; May 29, 1919. Grey Collection, Zane Grey, Inc. Unless otherwise noted, further citations of Grey letters and diaries are from material at Zane Grey, Inc.

17. The transition from manuscript to printed page caused Grey some anguish. Harper's wanted him to shorten *Wanderer of the Wasteland* by three thousand words. Grey ultimately complied with the request, but not before expressing a rather strong opinion. He asked Harper's: "What do you suppose Conrad would say to such a proposition, or Tarkington?" He reminded the publishers that they rejected his first five efforts, all of which were ultimate successes. Grey to Dolly Grey, July 6, 1922; *Diary*, October 22, 1923.

18. Burton Rascoe, Review of *Wanderer of the Wasteland, New York Tribune*, January 21, 1923, p. 19. Also, "New York's Awe at the Best Seller," *Literary Digest*, 76 (March 10, 1923), pp. 30-31.

19. T. K. Whipple, "American Sagas," *Zane Grey, The Man and his Works*, p. 25.

20. Loren Baritz, *City on a Hill* (New York, 1964), pp. 261-66.

21. Discussions of this fascinating tribe of Indians are in Henry Bamford Parkes, *A History of Mexico*, 3rd ed. (Boston, 1966), pp. 79, 296. See also Howard F. Cline, *dMexico, Revolution to Evolution, 1940-1960* (New York, 1963), p.73, and Charles G. Cumberland, *Mexico, The Struggle for Modernity* (New York, 1968), p. 200.

22. Grey to Murphy, July 21, 1912. Markham Collection.

23. L. H. Robbins, Review of *The Call of the Canyon, Zane Grey, The Man and His Works*, p. 52.

24. *Ibid.*, p. 54.

25. This book was first called *The Shores of Lethe*, various versions of which were written well before American involvement in World War I. On November 29, 1921, Grey wrote in his diary that he wanted the book to embody everything that was wrong with modern times. Later he changed the title to *Return of the Beast*, and still later to *The Day of the Beast*. He rewrote the book at least five times. When it was finally published, Dolly wrote to Grey, June 27, 1922: "You cannot expect 'Day of the Beast' to be liked . . . . It will hurt you with some of your readers & you will get a lot of protestations. But they'll swing back to you again . . . . This book shows versatility at least."

26. "Writer of the Range," *MD*, 13 (February, 1969), p. 202.

Chapter Three

1. Grey to Daniel Murphy, June 2, no year, Markham Collection.

2. "Popular Novels and Short Stories," *Review of Reviews* (June, 1912), p. 762.

3. Review of *Riders of the Purple Sage*, *Nation*, 94 (February 15, 1912), 161.

4. "A God [sic] Novel," *New York Times*, 17:82 (February 18, 1912).

5. Romer Grey (Zane's brother) to Grey, March 12, 1913.

6. "More to Come," *The New Yorker*, (July 19, 1950), pp. 17-18.

7. Grey visited the area in 1913, and said of it: "Sound, movement, life seemed to have no fitness here. Ruin was there and desolation and decay. The meaning of the ages was flung at me. A man became nothing." Grey, "Non-nezoshe, The Rainbow Bridge," *Recreation* 2 (New Series, February, 1915) LII, 63-67. Joe Lee, a Mormon cowboy, helped John Wetherill guide Grey to the area. Lee was a character (Lake) in *The Rainbow Trail*. The influenza epidemic of 1918 killed him. Grey lamented his passing: "He was a fine big-hearted Mormon cowboy and one whom I had great admiration for. I can see the lonely cabin on the bleak desert where he must have fought this Spanish influenza, as he fought everything, like a man. He was alone. He did not give up until overpowered by death. Alas! the sadness, the tragedy of it. . . . I hear the coyotes, the mournful wind sweeping the sand, the silence of the waste places! Another of my men of the open, gone to the great unknown." *Diary*, December 17, 1918.

8. Dolly Grey to Grey, August 18, 1915.

9. Modern Library Edition, p. 508.

10. Several critics faulted Grey for using unreal dialect in his novels. The only unreal thing, however, about *Under The Tonto Rim* is that the usual Western drawl is missing. Why he chose to employ "straight language" in this novel is unknown. Some typical quaint sayings of the West that Grey used in other novels were: to show anger: "Don't that make you so mad you want to spit all over yourself?"; to show intelligence: "He must of swallowed a dictionary onct," to denote a hopeless situation: "It's Katy-bar-the-door"; to express amazement: "By the great Horn-Spoon."; to show darkness: "It's darkern' the milltail of Hades."; and to show hospitality to horse-riding visitors: "Get down and come in." Critics who insisted that these and similar expressions used by Grey were unreal merely proved their lack of familiarity with the Western regions.

11. Henry Hoyns to Grey, December 12, 1925.

12. *Diary*, December 20, 1911.

13. A typed copy of this play is in the Grey Collection, Library of Congress.

14. Grey to Dolly Grey, undated.

15. Grey wrote a mountain novel, set in the Tonto, about another "discovery" —the production of "white mule," or illegal whiskey. He wrote much of the novel in 1926 while on an expedition to New Zealand and the South Seas. The book concerned the "Lilley-Hathaway feud" over sorghum rustling and "rights" to the output of "white mule." The work's title was changed and published in 1958 as *Arizona Clan*.

16. Grey to Robert Hobart Davis, March 6, 1915. Davis Papers, New York Public Library.

17. Grey to Romer Grey (Zane's son) March 18, 1937.

18. Dolly Grey to Grey, June 2, 1937.

19. Grey to Henry Hoyns, October 2, 1939. Grey Collection, Harper's.

20. Grey mentions Jones in *Tales of Lonely Trails*, Grossett-Dunlap Edition, pp. 240-41.

21. Ruby Johnson to Grey, undated. Zane Grey, Inc.

22. Edith Berry to Grey, undated. Zane Grey, Inc.

23. *Diary*, January 11, 1920.

Chapter Four

1. Grey's handwritten tribute, not only to Doyle, but to Ripley Hitchcock (to whom he dedicated *The U.P. Trail*), is in the Grey Collection, Library of Congress.

2. In a historical novel, the events are the major consideration. The characters are guided by these events, and are, therefore, subordinate to them.

3. Outline of *The U.P. Trail*, Grey Collection, Library of Congress.

4. Slingerland typified all those who hated the "shining steel band of progress connecting East and West." In this respect, he agreed with Nathaniel Hawthorne, who wrote in 1844: "There is the whistle of the locomotive—. . . . No wonder that it gives such a startling shriek, since it brings the noisy world into the midst of our slumbrous peace." See Leo Marx, *The Machine in the Garden* (New York, 1967), pp. 13-14.

5. *Diary*, February 15, 1918.

6. Grey to Ripley Hitchcock, February 20, 1918.

7. Grey to Anna Andre, February 16, 1918.

8. *Diary*, April 3, 1917.

9. *Diary*, December 29, 1918.

10. The original manuscript of *The Desert of Wheat* is in the Grey Collection, Library of Congress.

11. Original MS, *The Desert of Wheat*, Library of Congress.

12. Theodore Brooke, Review of *The Desert of Wheat*, *Harper's Magazine*, 825 (February, 1919).

13. *Diary*, November 23, 1921.

14. Dolly Grey to Grey, March 17, 1920.

15. Jean Kerr, *Zane Grey, Man of the West: A Biography* (New York, 1949), p. 204.

16. Grey to Dolly Grey, February 27, 1924.

17. This feud was also the basis for Dane Coolidge's, *The Men Killers*. Coolidge was a frequent critic of Grey, saying that the West he created was not realistic. For additional information on the Graham-Tewksbury feud, see Joe B. Frantz and Julian E. Choate, Jr., *The American Cowboy* (Norman, Oklahoma, 1955), pp. 111-14.

18. Theodore Brooke, Review of *To The Last Man*, "The Bookshelf," *Harper's Magazine* (February, 1922).

19. *Diary*, June 4-5, 1923.

20. Zane Grey, undated note to *Boy's Magazine*, Zane Grey, Inc.

21. Grey to Dolly Grey, July 8, 1923.

22. William H. Briggs to Zane Grey, May 16, 1925.

23. Grey did actual research for his book on a Navajo Reservation. There is no Nopah tribe of Indians.

24. *Diary*, June 24, 1922.

25. Burton W. Carrie to William H. Briggs, August 22, 1923. Zane Grey, Inc.

26. Grey to Dolly Grey, June 21, 1924.

27. Grey to Dolly Grey, March 16, 1924.

28. Grey to Dolly Grey, August 17, 1924.

29. Grey to William H. Briggs, May 23, 1924.

30. *Ibid.*

31. Grey to Lucien Hubbard, July 31, 1924.

32. It is 726 feet high, 660 feet long at the base, and 1,224 feet long at the top. It created Lake Mead the largest artificial body of water in the world.

33. Grey to Romer Grey, July 20, 1934.

34. Much of the plot for *Boulder Dam* was inspired by the existence of the white-slave traffic in and around Las Vegas while the dam was being constructed. The leading female character, Anne Vandergrift, after reading an advertisement for a job in a Los Angeles newspaper, went to Las Vegas and was threatened by a shite-slave operation. At the time Grey wrote *Boulder Dam*, he was intently reading Albert Londres, *The Road to Buenos Ayres* (1928), which dealt with white-slave traffic. Romer Grey to Evan Thomas, June 27, 1962. Grey Collection, Harper's.

Chapter Five

1. Grey to Dolly Grey, February 13, 1917.

2. Clayton Hamilton, *Manual of Fiction* (Garden City, 1924), pp. 3-20.

3. Grey to Dolly Grey, March 19, 1922.

4. Grey to Dolly Grey, August 7, 1922.

5. Another story, "Lighting," could possibly be put into this category, but it was about a wild horse who, far from ever really loving humans, spent most of his time eluding them. When he was finally captured, his captors were so enthralled by his greatness that they decided not to hand him over for the reward which had been offered. "Lightning" did not possess fidelity to man, as Jenet and Wildfire did.

6. Grey's first year of being on the best-selling lists was 1915, with *The Lone Star Ranger*. The last time was 1924, with *The Call of The Canyon*. His nine books on the list put him on a par with Booth Tarkington. Only Mary Roberts

Rinehart, with eleven best sellers, and Sinclair Lewis, with ten, exceeded Grey. See Alice Payne Hackett, *70 Years of Best-Sellers*, 1895-1965 (New York, 1967), p. 7.

7. Grey to Henry Hoyns, November 8, 1927.

8. Grey to Dolly Grey, August 19, 1929.

9. *The Zane Grey Collector*, Vol 2, No. 2, p. 9. Hackett, p. 87, gives the number sold at 2,087,837.

10 Grey to Dolly Grey, January 29, 1924.

11. *The Last of the Plainsmen*, p. 137.

12. In 1930 Arizona passed a law regulating the hunting of wild animals. Grey believed that his novels had done more than anything else to make Arizona a popular tourist state. He felt, therefore, that he should be exempt from the new hunting law. When the state government refused to make an exception of Grey, he left the state and never returned. He continued to write stories and novels, however, with Arizona settings.

13. Grey originally set *Horse Heaven Hill* in the 1920's. The book was not published until 1959, however, twenty years after Grey died. To maintain the "Zane Grey image," the time was set back by the publishers to the 1880's and 1890's. Doing so caused the book to be poor in comparison with most of the other Grey works. Besides, Grey set many of his most successful novels in the 1920's: *Call of the Canyon*, *The Shepherd of Guadaloupe*, and *Desert of Wheat*, to name three. These certainly did not hurt his image.

14. Grey to Romer Grey (Zane's son), April 2, 1937.

15. As early as 1904, Grey took Dolly's advice and started carrying a notebook around with him—in the manner of Robert Louis Stevenson, whom Grey greatly admired—in which to record his thoughts. Dolly told Grey to "take the commonest objects and write one or two little themes every day. They needn't be more than a few words, but make everyone of those few words count for a great deal. Learn to say just what you mean in the most concise way possible." Dolly Grey to Grey, June 8, 1904.

16. J. A. Wiborn, "Tribute to Grey," [[1924?]]. Grey Collection, Zane Grey, Inc.

17. *Diary*, November 23, 1920.

Chapter Six

1. John D. Hicks, *A Short History of American Democracy* (Boston, 1946), p. 506.

2. William Chenery to Dolly Grey, December 22, 1932.

3. Harry Burton to Dolly Grey, March 6, 1933.

4. At first, Brazos Keene was called "Pecos Smith." The name was changed in deference to another of Grey's novels, *West of the Pecos*.

5. Grey to Henry Hoyns, October 2, 1939. Grey Collection, Harper's.

6. Dolly Grey to Grey, June 30, 1933.

7. Dolly Grey to Grey, March 13, 1933.

8. The original manuscript of *Raiders of Spanish Peaks* is in the Grey Collection, Library of Congress.

9. Philip Durham and Everett L. Jones, *The Negro Cowboys* (New York, 1965), p. 1.

10. Perhaps the lack of unity was indicated by all the absentminded drawings and "doodles" on the back of several pages of the manuscript of *West of the Pecos*. The original copy is in the Grey Collection, Library of Congress.

11. Many reviews of Grey's books were ludicrous in that the reviewers adopted a high-blown "Western" jargon that was misleading. *The Maverick Queen* was reviewed by *Time* on June 19, 1950. The review took a minor incident (the shoot-out between Lincoln Bradway and "Gun Haskel") and treated it as the major event. The review also implied that "Gun Haskel" was the leading character in the novel.

12. Grey to Dolly Grey, September 27, 1928.

13. Still another novel about the operation of a ranch was *The Dude Ranger,* serialized by *McCall's* in 1930. It was, of course, about an Easterner taking over a ranch and rather hurriedly "learning the ropes."

14. Dolly Grey to Grey, June 17, 1936.

15. Doing so, however, turned attention away from the South, rendered economically prostrate by the Civil War. With investors preferring cattle to cotton, the post-war reclamation of the South was hindered. See William A. Harris, *Presidential Reconstruction in Mississippi*, (Baton Rouge, 1967), p. 162.

16. This book was one of Grey's more successful creations. Through 1951, its domestic sales came to 835,750 copies.

17. Another Grey manuscript, *The Fugitive Trail*, not published until 1957, dealt with the Cain-Abel thesis in which a man took the blame for his brother's crime, and eluded Texas Rangers for several years. The plot was very thin, and the characters were wooden. The book caused one English reader to inquire if it had been ghosted; it had been meticulously edited.

18. "My Answer to the Critics," no date, Zane Grey, Inc.

19. The original manuscript of *Fighting Caravans* is in the Grey Collection, Library of Congress.

20. William Chenery to Dolly Grey, July 2, 1931.

21. The Yaquis were discussed in Grey's novel, *Desert Gold*. See pp. 43-45.

22. Grey wrote another, less popular, book about Western cowboys in modern settings: *Wyoming* was first called *The Young Runaway*, and was serialized in 1932 in *Pictorial Review*. Its theme was the familiar one of an Easterner finding happiness in the West.

23. Dolly Grey to Grey, February 12, 1923.

24. John E. Pickett to Grey, February 27, 1923.

Chapter Seven

1. Grey to Dolly Grey, October 22, 1922.

2. No. 2, Vol. 16, pp. 217-24.

3. Dolly Grey to Grey, September 25, 1916.

4. Other short stories of Grey's not discussed in the text included "From Missouri," "Tigre," "The Horse Thief" (first called "The Outlaws of Palouse"), "The Rubber Hunter," and "Strange Partners of Twofold Bay." The last story was printed first in 1955 by *The American Weekly*. Another story, "The Adventures of Finspot," never published, was a story for little children about a small fish who

learned the lessons of survival among predatory fishes. The importance of parental supervision of children was an undercurrent of this story.

5. "Monty Price's Nightingale" was published by *Popular Magazine*, May 7, 1915, pp. 111-19.

6. The typewritten manuscript of "Amber's Mirage" is in the Grey Collection, The Library of Congress.

7. The typewritten manuscript of this play is in the Grey Collection, The Library of Congress.

8. The typewritten manuscript of this play is in the Grey Collection, The Library of Congress.

9. *Diary*, June 5, no year.

10. Later, Grey owned other, more sophisticated fishing boats, One was the *Gladiator*. In 1943, the ship, *Zane Grey*, was christened.

11. Review of *Tales of Fishes, Boston Transcript*, September 3, 1919, p. 8.

12. Review of *Tales of Fishes, New York Times*, October 26, 1919.

13. Theodore Brooke, Review of *Tales of Fishes, Harper's Magazine*, 831 (August, 1919).

14. R. H. Davis to Grey, September 3, 1919. Davis Collection.

15. Review of *Tales of Southern Rivers, Springfield Republican*, November 23, 1924, p. 5a.

16. *Diary*, January 1-5, 1926.

17. Grey to Dolly Grey, December 31, 1925.

18. Grey to Dolly Grey, January 19, 1926.

19. R. H. Davis to Grey, November 23, 1926. Davis Collection.

20. Grey visited Australia for the last time in 1939. In planning for the trip, he was intensely excited: "I can get a lot of magnificent material, some of it for fiction, and particularly I can round out the motion picture that I want to use on my lecture trip. . . . I know that trip will be hard work, but I am simply crazy to do it. . . . I will get a tremendous kick out of appearing before these audiences and of autographing books in big stores." Grey to Hoyns, October 10, 1938. Grey Collection, Harper's.

21. One reader of Grey's fishing books was Ernest Hemingway, who once turned down an offer from Grey for a joint fishing extravaganza, believing, apparently, that Grey wanted to ride to fame on his reputation. Hemingway's biographer, Carlos Baker, calls this thought "the silliest of surmises." See Carlos Baker, *Ernest Hemingway, A Life Story* (New York, 1969), p. 271.
p. 271.

In the first part of 1930 Grey fished for eighty-three days in Tahiti without a strike. On the eighty-fourth day he caught, with rod and reel, a giant Tahitian marlin that weighed 1,040 pounds. Trying desperately to get the creature ashore, Grey's fish was ravaged by sharks. Some Grey fans today credit Grey's experience with inspiring Hemingway's *The Old Man and the Sea*. See Grey, *Tales of Tahitian Waters*, 1931; and *The Zane Grey Collector*, Vol. 3, No. 1, pp. 12-13.

22. An instructive article on Grey's life as a sportsman is Robert H. Boyle's "The Man Who lived Two Lives in One," in *Sports Illustrated* (April, 1968), pp. 70-82.

23. Dolly Grey to R. H. Davis, August 23, 1929. Davis Collection.

24. Grey to Dolly Grey, March 16, 1927.

25. Grey to Dolly Grey, April 12, 1927.

26. *The Zane Grey Collector*, Vol. 3, No. 1, p. 3.

27. *Tales of Fresh Water Fishing*, p. 108.

28. Zane Grey, "Bonefish," *Field & Stream*, (August, 1918), pp. 297-302.

29. See Grey, "Avalon, the Beautiful," *Field & Stream* (May, 1918).

30. See *Sports Afield*, July, 1933; January and August, 1934; May and June, 1935.

31. See *Sports Afield*, January, 1962.

Chapter Eight

1. Margaret McOmie, "Zane Grey's Home as Exquisite Natural Beauty," *Better Homes and Gardens*, (March, 1928), p. 28.

2. See p. 28.

3. *Diary*, October 1, 1905.

4. *Diary*, August 8, 1910.

5. *Diary*, May 20, 1917.

6. *Diary*, October 1, 1905.

7. *Ibid.*

8. *Ibid.*

9. *Ibid.*

10. Grey to Daniel Murphy, undated. Markham Collection.

11. Grey to Murphy, undated. Markham Collection.

12. *Diary*, April 30, 1917.

13. Dolly Grey to Grey, March 12, 1920.

14. *Diary*, April 23, 1917.

15. See Charlotte Watkins Smith, *Carl Becker: On History and the Climate of Opinion* (Cornell, 1955).

16. *Diary*, April 7, 1917.

17. *Diary*, April 5, 1917.

18. Thomas Wells to Grey, April 23, 1919.

19. Grey to Dolly Grey, July 8, 1918.

20. Grey to Dolly Grey, February 14, 1922.

21. Dolly Grey to Robert H. Davis, January 4, 1935. Davis Collection.

22. Dolly Grey to Davis, January 4, 1935. Davis Collection.

23. Robert H. Davis to Dolly Grey, June 3, 1935. Davis Collection.

24. Dolly Grey to Grey, May 18, 1922.

25. Grey to Dolly Grey, November 27, 1928.

26. Grey to Henry Hoyns, October 2, 1939. Grey Collection, Harper's.

27. William Clark, to the writer, November 13, 1969. See William Clark, "Faust and Grey: A Study," *The Zane Grey Collector*, Vol. 2, No. 4, p. 3 See also Robert Easton, *Max Brand: The Big Westerner* (Norman, Oklahoma, 1970).

28. He was, for example, the creator of the "Dr. Kildare" series.

29. There are several lists showing the movies that were made of Grey's works. The best seems to be that of G. M. Farley in *The Zane Grey Collector*, Vol. 4, No. 4., with additions by Dale E. Case. Those novels which have been filmed at least four times include: *Riders of the Purple Sage, The Light of Western Stars, The Lone Star Ranger,* and *The Mysterious Rider.* Filmed at least three times were: *Heritage of the Desert, The Border Legion, Desert Gold, Nevada, The Last Trail, The Rainbow Trail, Sunset Pass, Under the Tonto Rim,* and *Wild Horse Mesa.* Jack Holt, Tim Holt, Randolph Scott, John Wayne, Robert Young, James Mason, "Buster" Crabbe, Dean Jagger, Scott Brady, Richard Arlen, Bebe Daniels, Lillian Leighton, Ann Sheridan, Wallace Beery, and Maureen O'Sullivan

were a few of the many stars in movies made from Zane Grey's books. Well over a hundred movies were based on Grey's writings.

30. See G. M. Farley, "E.R.B. and Zane Grey," *The Zane Grey Collector*, Vol. 2, No. 3, p. 3.

31. See Ivan A. Conger, "James Oliver Curwood, Son of the Forest," *The Zane Grey Collector*, Vol. 3, No. 1, p. 7.

32. *Diary*, January 24, 1920.

33. *Diary*, October 25, 1917.

34. *Diary*, October 11, 1932.

35. *Diary*, June ? , 1921.

36. Grey to Dolly Grey, August 29, 19??.

37. Zane Grey, "My Answer to the Critics," unpublished essay, Zane Grey, Inc.

38. *Ibid.*

39. Through 1951, *Riders of the Purple Sage* had domestic sales totaling 1,035,750; *The Light of Western Stars*, 995,600; and *Wildfire*, 926,250.

40. Tom Curry, "Zane Grey," *The Zane Grey Collector*, Vol. 5, No. 18, p. 10.

41. Henry Hoyns to Dolly Grey, November 18, 1939. Grey Collection, Harper's.

42. Dolly Grey to Daniel Beard, November 26, 1939. Beard Papers, Library of Congress.

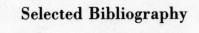

Selected Bibliography

Selected Bibliography

NOTE: Unless otherwise indicated, page numbers of Grey's books referred to in the text, are from Grossett-Dunlap editions.

PRIMARY SOURCES

1. *Books*. (Numbers in map correspond to numbers after some novels in the following list. They show the main setting of the novel.)

An American Angler in Australia. New York: Harper, 1937.
Arizona Ames. New York: Harper, 1932. (45).
Arizona Clan. New York: Harper, 1958. (16).
Betty Zane. New York: Charles Francis Press, 1903.
Black Mesa. New York: Harper, 1955. (1).
Blue Feather and other Stories., New York: Harper, 1961. (46).
Boulder Dam. New York: Harper, 1963. (30).
Captives of the Desert. New York: Harper, 1952. (2).
Desert Gold. New York: Harper, 1913. (3).
Don. New York: Harper, 1928.
Fighting Caravans. New York: Harper, 1929. (47).
Forlorn River. New York: Harper, 1927. (38).
Horse Heaven Hill. New York: Harper, 1959. (39).
Ken Ward in the Jungle. New York: Harper, 1959. (39).
Kinghts of the Range. New York: Harper, 1939. (48).
Lost Pueblo. New York: Harper, 1954. (4).
Majesty's Rancho. New York: Harper, 1942. (5).
Man of the Forest. New York: Harper, 1920. (17).
Nevada. New York: Harper, 1928. (40).
Raiders of Spanish Peaks. New York: Harper, 1938. (49).
Riders of the Purple Sage. New York: Harper, 1912. (18).
Robber's Roost. New York: Harper, 1932. (19).
Rogue River Feud. New York: Harper, 1948. (31).
Roping Lions in the Grand Canyon. New York: Harper, 1924. (6).
Shadow on the Trail. New York: Harper, 1946. (50).
Spirit of the Border. New York: A. L. Burt, co., 1906.

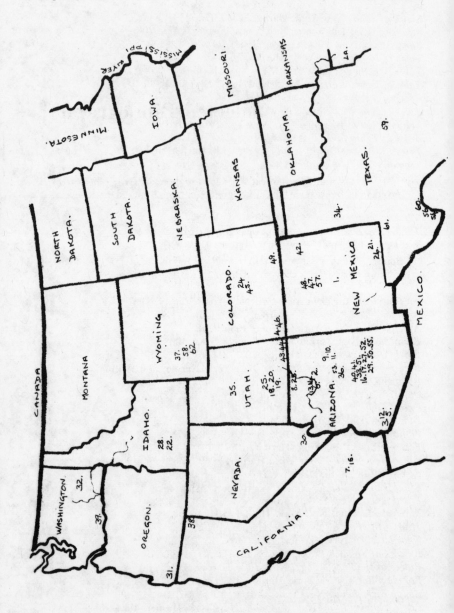

Stairs of Sand. New York: Harper, 1943. (7).
Stranger From The Tonto. New York: Harper, 1956. (20).
Sunset Pass. New York: Harper, 1931. (21).
Tales of Fishes. New York: Harper, 1919.
Tales of Fishing Virgin Seas. New York: Harper, 1925.
Tales of Fresh Water Fishing. New York: Harper, 1928.
Tales of Lonely Trails. New York: Harper, 1922. (8).
Tales of Southern Rivers. New York: Harper, 1924.
Tales of Swordfish and Tuna. New York: Harper, 1927.
Tales of Tahitian Waters. New York: Harper, 1931.
Tales of the Angler's Eldorado. New York: Harper, 1926.
Tappan's Burro and other Stories. New York: Harper, 1923. (41).
The Border Legion. New York: Harper, 1916. (22).
The Call of the Canyon. New York: Harper, 1924. (9).
The Code of the West. New York: Harper, 1934. (51).
The Day of the Beast. New York: Harper, 1922.
The Deer Stalker. New York: Harper, 1949. (23).
The Desert of Wheat. New York: Harper, 1919. (32).
The Drift Fence. New York: Harper, 1933. (52).
The Dude Ranger. New York: Harper, 1951. (53).
The Fugitive Trail. New York: Harper, 1957. (54).
The Hash Knife Outfit. New York: Harper, 1933. (55).
The Heritage of the Desert. New York: Harper, 1910. (10).
The Last Trail. New York: A. L. Burt, Co., 1906.
The Last of the Plainsmen. New York: Outing Publishers, 1908. (11).
The Light of Western Stars. New York: Harper, 1914. (12).
The Lone Star Ranger. New York: Harper, 1915. (56).
The Lost Wagon Train. New York: Harper, 1936. (57).
The Maverick Queen. New York: Harper, 1950. (58).
The Mysterious Rider. New York: Harper, 1921. (24).
The Ranger and other Stories. New York: Harper, 1961.
The Rainbow Trail. New York: Harper, 1915. (25).
The Redheaded Outfield and other Stories. New York: Harper, 1920.
The Shepherd of Guadaloupe. New York: Harper, 1930. (26).
The Short Stop. New York: Harper, 1909.
The Trail Driver. New York: Harper, 1936. (59).
The Thundering Herd. New York: Harper, 1918. (34).
The U.P. Trail. New York: Harper, 1918. (35).
The Vanishing American. New York: Harper, 1925. (36).
The Wilderness Trek. New York: Harper, 1944.
The Wolf Tracker. New York: Harper, 1930.
The Young Forester. New York: Harper, 1910. (13).
The Young Lion Hunter. New York: Harper, 1911. (14).
The Young Pitcher. New York: Harper, 1911.
30,000 On The Hoof. New York: Harper, 1940. (27).
Thunder Mountain. New York: Harper, 1935. (28).
To The Last Man. New York: Harper, 1922. (33).

Twin Sombreros. New York: Harper, 1941. (60).
Under the Tonto Rim. New York: Harper, 1926. (29).
Valley of Wild Horses. New York: Harper, 1947. (42).
Wanderer of the Wasteland. New York: Harper, 1923. (15).
West of the Pecos. New York: Harper, 1937. (61).
Western Union. New York: Harper, 1939. (37).
Wildfire. New York: Harper, 1917. (43).
Wild Horse Mesa. New York: Harper, 1928. (44).
Wyoming. New York: Harper, 1953. (62).
Zane Grey's Adventures in Fishing (ed. Ed Zern) New York: Harper, 1952.
Zane Grey's Book of Camps and Trails. New York: Harper, 1931.
Zane Grey Omnibus. New York: Harper, 1943.

2. *MSS*.

Daniel Beard Collection, Library of Congress, Washington, D.C.
Robert Hobart Davis Collection, New York Public Library.
Zane Grey Collection, Harper & Row. (A private collection, not generally available to the public.)
Zane Grey Collection, Library of Congress, Washington, D.C.
Zane Grey Collection, University of Texas, Austin.
Zane Grey Collection, Zane Grey, Inc. (A private collection, not generally available to the public.)
Edwin Markham Collection, Wagner College, Staten Island, New York.

3. *Articles in Periodicals*. (This is a highly selective list of articles, designed primarily to show the different categories of subjects in Grey's articles.)

'Big Game Fishing in New Zealand Seas," *Science America*, CXXXIX (August, 1928), 116-18.
"Breaking Through, The Story of My Own Life," *American Magazine* 98 (July, 1924), 11-13.
"Down Into the Desert," *Ladies' Home Journal*, XLI (January, 1924), 8-9.
"Record Fight With a Swordfish," *Country Life*, XXXVIII (August, 1920), 33-7.
"The Man Who Influenced Me Most," *American Magazine*, CII (August, 1926), 52-55.
"What the Desert Means to Me," *American Magazine*, XCVIII (November, 1924), 5-8.

SECONDARY SOURCES

DURHAM, PHILIP and JONES, EVERETT. *The Negro Cowboys*. New York: Dodd, Mead & Co., 1965. Valuable for its insights into an often neglected phase of Western history, a phase that Grey discussed more than most Western novelists of his time.

EASTON, ROBERT. *Max Brand, The Big Westerner*. Norman: University of Oklahoma, 1970. Excellent biography of Brand, one of Grey's contemporaries in writing Western novels.

EASTON, ROBERT and BROWN, MACKENZIE. *Lord of Beasts, The Life of Buffalo Jones*. Tucson: University of Arizona Press, 1961. Study of the highly interesting Buffalo Jones; several pages are devoted to Zane Grey.

GOBLE, DANNY G. "Zane Grey's West: An Intellectual Reaction." Unpublished M.A. Thesis, University of Oklahoma, 1969. Useful study of Grey's impact upon American literature.

GRUBER, FRANK. *Zane Grey*. Cleveland: World Publishers, 1970. This overwritten account of Grey's life is somewhat better than the earlier biography of Grey by Jean Kerr because Gruber had access to materials that Kerr did not. Still, Gruber's biography is loosely organized and does not sufficiently heed the motives behind Grey's writings.

HALEY, J. EVETTS. *Charles Goodnight, Cowman and Plainsman*. Norman: University of Oklahoma Press, 1936. A well-written, informative account of one of "Buffalo" Jones's competitors in the production of "cattalo."

KERR, JEAN. *Zane Grey, Man of the West*. New York: Grossett and Dunlap, 1949. Poorly written, this book discusses mostly the trips that Grey took but not very many of the books he wrote.

MCKNIGHT, CHARLES. *Our Western Border*. Cincinnati: J. C. McCurdy & Co., 1876. This volume was highly important to Grey in his early writing career. It contains several hair-raising episodes of life along the early Virginia frontier. Grey said he knew this book by heart.

SCHNEIDER, NORRIS F. *Zane Grey "The Man Whose Books Made the West Famous,"* Zanesville, Ohio: By the Author, 1967. Informative booklet about Grey by a man who spent many years studying Grey's career.

SCOTT, KENNETH W., "The Heritage of the Desert: Zane Grey Discovers the West," *Markham Review*, II (February, 1970), 10-15. Well-written article on the novel that was Grey's first major success.

Zane Grey, The Man and his Works. (a compilation) New York: Harper & Brothers, 1928. A valuable collection of articles either by Grey or about him.

Index

Index